What Would the Sage Do Now?

A Spiritual Approach to Problem Solving

GALA GORMAN

MetaComm Media
Boulder, Colorado 80304

Gorman, Gala.
What Would the Sage Do Now? / by Gala Gorman.
Includes index.
ISBN 0-9711375-0-1
1. Self-help 2. Spirituality 3. Metaphysical studies 4. Creative problem-solving

Editor/Interior Design: *Michele Rousseau*
Cover Design: *Bob Dempsey*

Printed in the United States of America

ISBN 0-9711375-0-1

METACOMM MEDIA
A division of MetaComm International, LLC
Boulder, CO 80304

On the World Wide Web at http://www.metacommintl.com

Acknowledgements

While everyone has served as a teacher in the process of preparing me to create this book, my father, Gale Gorman, was responsible not only for bringing me into this world but for exposing me to astrology and 'thought' management. I am fortunate to have a supportive, believing friend in him.

Michele Rousseau has been a valued associate for a couple of years now. Her skillful craftsmanship is evident on every page of the book, as she was the person solely responsible for editing this work. I have told her before, and will tell her here, that this book would not be what it is today without her assistance. She gave her heart and soul, and I am grateful.

My friend, Valarie Hufft, was a great resource as I began to wholeheartedly study this subject. When we are together, the veil between the worlds parts, and magick is created. Knowing her has been a blessing in my life.

I thank every person that has contributed in some way on my path. There isn't room to name everyone, but know that I appreciate every experience.

Lastly, I thank you for taking the leap of faith and putting your toe in the water by choosing to read this book. You are embarking on a journey that will profoundly change your life. I love the company - the more, the merrier!

Table of Contents

Introduction

I don't know where it all started. Maybe it just started with a feeling of discomfort, like wanting to crawl out of my own skin. As a Certified Public Accountant, I was at a point where I was looking for greater meaning in life and knew I needed to make a change. And change I have! Sometimes I start to recall my life ten years ago and then realize I can't really recall it at all. It's been an incredible journey.

At this point, I have achieved considerable personal growth by embracing a metaphysical approach and finding balance in my life. I have learned the value of balancing my physical, spiritual, and emotional aspects and of using all the resources available to me in this life. I know now that metaphysical approaches can not only co-exist with, but greatly enhance, one's success in business, as well as in life overall.

It has been a long road. If I have read less than 50 books in the last ten years, I would be surprised. And while each one contributed to my learning and growth, what seemed to be missing was the synthesized version. The part that involves *how* you incorporate the principles into your daily life. That was my inspiration for this book – to provide the direction that seemed to be missing in my search for greater meaning and to facilitate your journey along this same path.

I have worked on the material for this book in earnest for several years now. For a long time, I didn't understand why it was taking me so long to complete it. Tackling big projects was not unfamiliar to me. This should have been no different. Yet it was.

About halfway through the book, I realized that I couldn't have written it a moment sooner. I needed every experience in order to feel prepared to share what I have learned with you so that I might be able to help reduce your learning curve. The guidance had to flow. It had to come from a place of wisdom and knowingness, rather than being merely ideas and concepts.

Throughout the book, you'll find key words that try to convey the wisdom I've gained. For example, I refer to 'Spirit', 'God', and 'the universe' interchangeably. It took a while for me, in my journey, to accept the concept of 'God' as a higher power, a source of wisdom and guidance, instead of as a symbol of organized religion. At that point, 'Spirit' seemed to be a more comfortable term. But, sometimes, even 'Spirit' doesn't seem to embrace the vastness that the term attempts to define. In times like these, I use 'the universe' to conceptualize how big the force is that stands at attention, ready to assist us as we move through life. So throughout this book, when you see references to 'God', 'Spirit', or 'the universe', understand that these names all represent the same, vast higher power available to each of us.

And then we come to 'magick'. I spell magick with a 'k' at the end to differentiate it from the illusions used by stage performers that involve sleight of hand. Magick is a function of harnessing the universal powers available to us all, in order to manifest the reality we want our lives to be. It is our ability to create our own miracles with focused intent and Spirit's guidance. When you open your heart and then follow the signs, or intuitive leads, that Spirit offers to you, you will find ample magick and miracles manifesting in your life.

Recognizing the miracles in your life is the single, most effective way to propel yourself through the process of spiritual growth and personal fulfillment. As I've come upon difficult places throughout the process, I have always found the miracle in some book or spoken word that propelled me through them and back onto the path.

Miracles come in all shapes and sizes. I've found that most don't present themselves in a spectacular way. They *ease* onto the scene, allowing you to incorporate them into your life and evolution. It can be something as simple as asking God for a little help with something and thanking him for the miracle when it presents itself.

I have come to trust that everything happens as it is meant to, that I will be exactly where I need to be at the time I need to be there. That, in itself, is truly a miracle - to be optimistically anxious about what's in store, instead of consumed with fear. In a way, it is like approaching life wearing rose-colored glasses. Everything takes on new meaning and is rewarding in ways that you could not have seen before.

The biggest hurdle to clear in pursuing this path is the covert, internal resistance that you will face. The subconscious mind is at work in everything you do, attempting to control things much of the time. The trick is to get past thinking you can suppress your subconscious and learn to embrace it. It is a level of your consciousness that, along with the conscious and super-conscious mind, makes life really interesting.

When I began this process over ten years ago, I thought it would be fairly easy to reprogram my subconscious. I figured that, since I knew that it was this part of myself that was causing the trouble and making the less-than-enlightened decisions, all I needed to do was get in there and take its power away. The more I grew to understand how the subconscious works, the more I realized I didn't know – and the larger the problem became.

Let's say you've seen a behavior pattern that you've recognized you must let go of in order to be the person you say you want to be. You didn't create a behavior pattern overnight. You spent years perfecting it. When you're feeling this vulnerable, you are likely to be compelled to do something – make some change – to move through it quickly. But you don't want to throw the baby out with the bath water.

If you really examine the behavior, you'll realize that it wasn't created just to trip you up. It has served you well in some area(s) of your life. You need to really work through the behavior and determine if you really want to get rid of it entirely. The only way a change will really permeate your life is if it is made *by* you, *for* you. It might take a special person in your life to show you a part of yourself that isn't helping you get to where you say you want to go, but you aren't really going to change for someone else. The change must be made for you. And even if you make the decision to change from this moment forward, you will still have the aftershock to deal with.

It can be helpful to have a counselor walk you through the process of reinventing yourself. A counselor can help you sit with the behavior, examine it from all angles, and determine what change will really benefit the whole you. The counselor can help you integrate the new you, by showing you where you've made progress and supporting you when you fall off the wagon.

When I went into counseling after my divorce, I was afraid that I would not be able to function in my life, as I knew it, after the work was done. Eventually, I got to the point with my first counselor where I didn't feel like I was making progress and I wanted to try hypnotherapy. It seemed really appealing at this point, to just go in and find out what was causing all the trouble. At that time, my first counselor recommended my second counselor to me.

The new counselor was all business. There was no candy-coating things with her. She helped me reprogram myself. It was tough work, and it took backbone to go through it. The spotlight was on my dysfunctional behavior patterns, and there was no way to avoid watching them move across the screen. It was a year of profound discoveries. I realized there are layers in my subconscious that I will probably never get to in this lifetime, but I have made so much progress. I realized that I had nothing to fear from counseling and everything to gain. I ended up with a new life that preserved all the functional parts of my old life and provided me with ways to be functional in the areas of my life that were dysfunctional before. In essence, I had it all.

At a certain point, I began to understand that I would get much further with my subconscious if I didn't try to force my will on it. It is a bit like what is referred to as 'child psychology'. I had to coerce my subconscious gently into my corner, especially when I was confronted with a problem. The bigger the problem seemed, the more chaotic things got. So I had to spend a lot of time convincing my subconscious that we could solve any problem with the universe's help. But why would the universe step in to help me? Doesn't it have better things to do?

That's when the S-A-G-E approach began to develop. If I asked myself "What would the sage do now?", it was easier to accept that the universe was available to someone of that social (and spiritual) standing. If I could tap into the wisdom of the sages, the universe was available to me. Eventually, it was easy for the subconscious to accept that I am a sage. We are all connected; we are all 'one'. In this way, I am the 'Wise Old Sage'. And so are you. My hope is that this book will help you access the wisdom of the sage for yourself. May your journey be wondrous!

Chapter 1
Know Yourself

"Familiarity breeds contempt."

I have spent years now talking to people about getting acquainted with themselves. More often than not, I find they are afraid of what they might discover. What familiar parts of their lives would they need to leave behind, if they really faced that they were living a life of quiet desperation?

The turning point for me came about ten years ago. I was unhappy with my life and thought it was primarily due to my relationship (or lack of relationship) with my husband. After many months of struggling with my conflicting emotions, I made the decision to leave the relationship and create a new life.

While that was a critical point in the process, the point of no return came about a year later, when the relationship I entered into after my marriage also failed. There was no denying that the only common denominator was *me*.

That was the beginning of the end of my former self. *"Nothing changes until I change; when I change, everything changes."* This first, courageous step is necessary for those who want to dig below the surface and find something truly meaningful.

While familiarity may breed contempt in some situations, familiarity is just what is required when it comes to knowing yourself and what makes you tick. That can be really scary.

As a result, risk is something you need to get pretty comfortable with. Any time you abandon something in your life, there is a risk that you will look back and say, "I sure wish I had made a different choice." So, before you let go of anything, spend plenty of time making sure that what you are releasing is something you feel you should have abandoned many moons ago. By the time you take the steps necessary to move in a different direction, you will be totally convinced that you are doing the right thing. It has yet to fail me.

I am an earth-sign person, with seven out of ten planets in earth signs. I'll leave the astrology lesson for a later chapter, but I can tell you that I would be really uncomfortable without both feet firmly planted on the ground and a warm, fuzzy security blanket in hand. When I make changes, I first consider the ramifications 12 ways to Sunday.

Over the last several years, I've taken a leap of faith over a would-be canyon several times. Once the action has been taken, there has been an incredible sense of relief and of knowing that I did the right thing. I haven't looked back – not a moment of regret. Not even a "Why didn't I do that sooner?"

In order to experience it just the way I did, I needed to turn over every stone. I needed to release what wasn't working gently, so that I could embrace what I was becoming.

The universe sends you situations and experiences that challenge you to take a closer look. If you can actually hurdle that bar, then you can figure out what to do with what you've discovered.

One of the ways you begin to understand yourself is by recognizing your behavior patterns. What are your overt personality traits or behaviors? Covert?

I recently attended a workshop, and we started talking about what makes a person 'fun'. I offered that I am not an overtly fun person, but I am covertly fun. There is a mischievous little elf inside of me that, given any outside stimuli, comes to the surface for the opportunity to play. It wouldn't be 'me' to be overtly fun. The serious, get-the-job-done side of me would be totally uncomfortable with that.

I know there is value in every part of me. And as long as I know who has come to the party, I can enjoy what they have brought to play with. It's when you resist what is presenting itself that you set off a time bomb. At some point, the unexpressed part of yourself will have to surface.

For instance, I am not naturally nice. Now, most people who know me would actually say that isn't true, so let me explain. It took me a long time to really own this and to accept myself just the way I am.

Some people just ooze kindness. No matter what the situation, they greet it with a charming non-confrontational approach. That is *not* me. When the situation requires it, I am plenty confrontational. I don't take "No" for an answer when there is a principle at stake, and I am willing to fight for what really matters to me. You can probably imagine that, in those situations, I am not very nice. If you're on the other end of the conversation, you are looking for a way to get rid of me.

To give you an example, I signed up for a long distance service plan that cost six cents a minute. When I got my bill, the provider had charged me 28 cents a minute. (I didn't even know they had plans for 28 cents per minute any more.) The first person I talked to told me that there were no records documenting my low-cost plan so I needed to pay the bill.

As you can imagine, this was not one of those situations where I practiced overt niceness. I thought of all the other people that had been taken advantage of because paperwork was supposedly missing. Sometimes being assertive and standing up for yourself is just what you need to do.

By the time I was finished dealing with this situation, the provider had made adjustments to my account for all of the excess charges. Plus, I had actually worked out a couple of other, totally-unrelated issues quite easily while dealing with the knowledgeable customer service representative.

The moral of the story? Problems are really opportunities, and everything happens for a reason. This will be the underlying theme for everything we look at.

"Leave no stone unturned."

Any problem you face can be looked at with an attitude of discovery. When I describe my life to people, I tell them it is like being on a treasure hunt every day. I am looking for messages and signs, filtering through alternatives, trying to get out of my own way. It never ceases to amaze me how beautifully orchestrated the universe is.

The masters might say that the truly enlightened aren't asking questions and are unaffected by watching the plan unfold. I guess, if that's the case, I'm not quite ready to go there. I delight in the process. It's fun. Sure I have moments where I am overwhelmed, but with the tools I have in my tool chest, I move through the discomfort quickly and emerge enlightened.

Of course, my view of the world might be a little different than most. I see things through the eyes of infinite possibilities. When you ask for something that might not be critical to your happiness – maybe just a daily convenience – and see how quickly it manifests, you can't help but translate that into bigger things. If you really believe that the universe supports you, then your only job is to figure out where you really want to be and go for it!

That's the key to knowing yourself. It isn't about what someone else wants for you. It's about what you want for yourself. We see this so often with kids. As parents, we have dreams of what our children will be from conception. Rather than nurturing our child's interests, we groom them to be what we want them to be. It's justifiable, isn't it? They deserve the benefit of our wisdom, right? After all, we only want 'the best' for them.

For example, all my niece really wanted for Christmas was a scooter. The adults got together and decided the kids needed a computer. For us, that was a huge gift, overshadowing every other gift. The problem was that *we* were the ones who wanted the kids to have a computer. The only thing my niece cared about was that she got a scooter. She knew what *she* wanted and that was what really mattered. If *you* don't dream your grandest dream, then how will the universe even know where to start in helping *you* create it?

Many of the things we dream of involve our enjoyment of life. I think we can all agree with the statement, "Time flies when you're having fun," and have had times in our lives when we have experienced the zone. But time didn't really fly. In fact, it stood still, almost like an out-of-body experience. We were totally unaware of what was going on in the moment. It was more about being a part of something in creation.

How do you find that excitement more often and make it a much larger part of your life experience? You can start by identifying your passions. What makes you angry, happy, sad, joyful? What restaurants do you like to frequent? What movies do you like to see?

I am a sucker for a romantic comedy. I must admit that my relationships have mirrored the romantic comedies I find so entertaining. In real life, though, they aren't quite as much fun.

What happens in a romantic comedy? Boy meets girl. Love at first sight. Something, someone, or geography keeps them apart. In the movie, nine times out of ten, they eventually find eternal bliss. I must admit, I am very disappointed when a screenwriter leaves us hanging at the end. I need my 'happily ever after' fix.

People will tell me that real life relationships aren't like the movies. I beg to differ. I think I can have 'happily ever after', if I can just get to the bottom of what it is in me that wants to keep recreating the story from the beginning. Obviously, I couldn't keep starting over if I actually found 'happily ever after'. This awareness, though, gives me a starting point for working toward success in a relationship.

"Failure breeds success."

You have to know black to know white, dark to know light, slow to know fast. I do agree it's true, but why is that? I saw something the other day that said: *"Once you experience the pain of accomplishment, all pain is endurable."* When you realize, with hindsight, the good that results when you persevere once, it is easier to find the strength and trust in the universe to meet the next challenge head-on.

I was in a bit of a rush one day and needed to mail a package that already had postage on it. My errand route wasn't going to take me near a post office before the last pick-up, so I asked the universe for a postal person to make themselves available on my route. Within seconds, I noticed that there was a mail truck two vehicles ahead of me. In a moment, the truck stopped, and I pulled in behind it, gratefully turning over responsibility for my package.

This might seem like a simple coincidental convenience to some. For me, it was a momentous occasion. At that instant, I realized that I could truly manifest whatever I needed in the blink of an eye – literally. The only thing missing in the formula is how to take the quantum leap from the small things (a mail truck) to something much larger (a major goal).

Every day, we are conditioning ourselves for what we expect life to be like. If we allow the manifestation of the small stuff to really sink in, it helps condition us to what is possible. The universe really *is* listening. All we need to do is communicate with it.

Personally, I talk to God every day. This isn't surprising. Anyone who has made a practice of prayer talks to God. And God talks back to me in many ways. The clearest way I've found is using a journal.

Julia Cameron wrote a book, The Artist's Way, that has had an enormous impact on people around the world. The cornerstone of working with the book is what Julia calls 'morning pages'. I won't go into detail, but I will say that the exercise has created nothing less than a miracle many times in my life. My journal is one of the most useful tools in my spiritual tool chest.

When I describe the process to people, I say it's like I am talking to myself, I am talking to God, and God is talking to me – in a pretty clever dialog. It is impossible to get too caught up in my own 'stuff' when I see it in written form. The "Aha's" come very quickly, and I move through sticking points with ease and grace.

The importance of using a disciplined approach to journaling can't be overlooked. It has taken me a while to truly honor the process. What you're trying to do here is peel the onion. You want to go deeper, to understand what is keeping you from having the life you've always dreamed of. There's no way to get this insight without confronting your subconscious head-on.

While there are many ways to do that – none of which are effortless – journaling is the least threatening. You are actively involved in 'doing' something, as opposed to the nothingness of meditation. You have a private audience with yourself since no one will see what you have written.

Some days I write things that I wouldn't want anyone else to read. Maybe I'm feeling confused or angry, and all the possibilities are poured onto the page. If someone involved were to read what I've written, it might be really threatening. Yet, when I'm done, I am so light. It's truly a freeing experience.

What I've come to realize is that, several days later (or maybe as soon as tomorrow), the situation has resolved itself perfectly for all concerned. It is the creative process that's important – actually critical – to the effectiveness.

Creativity is the by-product of having space in your life to birth something that comes from the heart. We all have busy, hectic schedules and very little time in our lives to make space for creating.

As a result, I spend virtually no time listening to or reading media. To me, watching television is a clear example of tuning *out*. In fact, I sometimes hear people discussing major events that I am completely oblivious to. At this point, I usually tune in to a hard news show that gives me the facts in a half hour so that I can get on with things that I consider a better use of my time. Since the focus here is on tuning *in*, I recommend that you too, challenge yourself to also wisely choose the time you spend with the television.

In order to get to know yourself, you have to spend time alone with 'me, myself and I'. No children, friends, spouses, associates – just yourself. I will admit that I take my dog with me a lot. I don't have to worry about his likes and dislikes affecting my process. That, on the other hand, would not work for my mother. She would be too concerned with the dog's needs to really spend time with herself.

It's all part of the process. When you get to know yourself, you learn to recognize the ways you escape your own process (and progress). You learn, too, the importance of loving yourself.

"To thine own self be true."

Most of us think we love ourselves, but actions speak louder than words (and thoughts). How do you spend your time every day? Are you doing things that feel supportive of your dreams and make you happy?

In this codependent-dependent society, you typically aren't rewarded for what you do for yourself, only what you do for others. Your own happiness is not particularly important. Yet, I'm sure you've been around people that are miserable. Nothing works out for them, and therefore they have an aura of negativity around them. This is devastating to anyone who enters their field. You can almost feel the life-blood draining out of you if you spend much time around them. When we are unhappy and living in misery, we are a drain on the other people in our lives. They may not be aware enough to label it, but it affects everyone and everything.

In order to have energy to give, you have to build up your own storehouse. You have to spend time developing the true primary relationship – the one with yourself. Some people might say that their relationship with God is the true primary relationship. I would counter that it is the same thing. Since God is within you, the only way to develop your spiritual foundation is to get to know yourself intimately.

Once you have that relationship, all the other ego-based relationships in your life assume their proper place.

At first, though, the people who depend on you may get scared when you really engage in the process of self-development and start making changes. When they start to resist the changes you make that ultimately affect them, how do you deal with the uncomfortable feelings that develop when you realize your choices are making those close to you unhappy? You focus on what's available to you once you start taking care of yourself. Once you are taken care of, you have so much more to offer everyone in your life. There is no other choice to be made. If you're genuine and honest in your communications, the people that love and depend on you will be more inclined to stay the course.

Of course, some of your friends may not fit into your life quite as well as they once did. But, true friends love you just the way you are. They want for you what *you* want for yourself, even if that means supporting you as you grow right out of the relationship.

"Birds of a feather flock together."

It can help to find others (outside of your immediate circle of family and friends) who are already doing things differently and who will be available to you as you enter the abyss. You will need to talk about things you're thinking and feeling that are just too close to home for those who share their lives with you. Sure, there are exceptions, and if you've been fortunate enough to find that, be grateful. For most of us, we're on different paths or in different stages and would really benefit from sharing with someone that is in a similar place.

I am human, and I like it that way. I'm not even going to try to pretend that I don't need relationships with other humans. Spending time with people who are working on themselves and who honor the enormous commitment that has been made is especially inspirational and uplifting. When you have an opportunity to experience this, you feel energized rather than drained. That is the point where you realize that you want to be a sail, not an anchor. In order to be that, you first have to live it.

It can also be tremendously transformational to work with a professional through different stages of the process. If you choose to work with someone, I urge you to make sure they understand what you're trying to accomplish and that their goal is to empower you, rather than create dependency.

In my case, the counselor I was seeing when I reached my 'point of no return' suggested that I go to Esalen. I have come to love this truly special place in Big Sur,

California, but my first time there was more than a little scary. I would have been happier to be a fish out of water. Now, I go to Esalen once or twice a year, and it has become a barometer check for me.

When I describe Esalen to people, what seems to paint the most accurate picture is that people there 'process for a living'. What I mean is that they focus on the self-development process every minute of every day. They speak a different language. The world exists as their stage for growth, and everything revolves around that.

I attended a group meeting several months ago, and the first thing I noticed is the difference in how people there communicate. They *feel* their way through it. Sometimes that can get a little ugly and uncomfortable along the way, but the results are amazing. Every conversation becomes an integral part of your own personal discovery process. It really doesn't matter what side of the conversation you're on.

Over the years, I've learned how to bring bits and pieces of Esalen into the light of day, using more genuine communication and truly honoring myself and my own process. When I do this, it is the greatest gift I give to others.

"You can't judge a book by its cover."

I receive plentiful gifts from others too. Relationships of any kind give you lots of material to work with. It's always easier to see what you don't like or don't want to be in another person.

Sometimes we deny that there is anything within us that is similar to what we don't like about another person. When this happens to me, I usually ask myself, *"How have I done the same thing that this annoying person has done? How are they like me?"* This is the time when you have to have compassion for yourself. It can be a pretty humbling experience to see something in others that isn't really pretty and then own it for yourself. You want to go crawl under a rock and hide.

This actually might be helpful for a little while; you need time to process it. Journal your way through it. Walk it off. Meditate, if that works for you. (I usually have too much energy to go straight to meditation.) What I will say is that no one – not even your most trusted advisor – has anything that would be valuable for you to hear at this point. The only one to commune with is yourself. It is at these moments that your greatest growth comes. If you're willing to go into it and explore it for all it's worth, the payoff is the equivalent of finding the next clue in the search for the hidden treasure.

The true defining moments don't come along that often, thank God. We couldn't handle a barrage of this kind of stuff. When they do present themselves, though, you need to take full advantage of them. *"How does this behavior serve me? How might I like to change the way I react to situations? What is the origin of the feelings I am experiencing?"* This is really juicy stuff. Recognizing when you're overreacting is the easiest way to find your pressure points.

If you're in a close relationship with someone that finds your behavior bewildering, you can tell them that you realize you're overreacting and you're trying to figure out exactly what is going on. Ask for a little time, and then honor them by coming back to it when you've had time to process it yourself. There is much to be learned for both of you when a conflict arises. We just have to accept that some people aren't ready to deal with the issues.

Once you've recognized that the person annoying you is actually yourself in a mirror, you are on your way to self-acceptance… *and* acceptance of others. Since nothing is all bad (or all good), you can immediately go to determining how the behavior serves you in certain situations.

Of course, sometimes this is easier said than done. When I find a characteristic in myself that just doesn't seem to be consistent with who I say I am becoming, I look for the common cause of the derailment. For me, it's stupid rules. Every organization has them. When confronted with a stupid rule, I ask, "Why do you do that?" More often than not, I get, "I don't make the rules, I only work here." If I actually got a decent explanation, I would happily comply. It is in the wake of ignorance that the 'less than nice' me emerges.

Why would you make it difficult to work with you for no apparent reason? If there is a compelling reason for the policy, wouldn't it be so obvious and important that it would be easily communicated by anyone in the organization? Most of the time, a stupid rule has been put into place as a result of some overreaction to a situation that would have been more easily handled if someone could just say, "That's the rule." It never really works that way, because the situation is never the same. By the time you try to apply the rule again to a special situation, it doesn't fit and there's really no history available to draw from.

Fortunately, I know myself well enough by now to be able to see a stupid rule reaction coming. I can decide if I want to confront it head on or if I need to preserve my energy for other battles. The 'old me' would have just gone into battle; the 'new me' *chooses* my battles.

Human imperfection is a grand thing. One person's flaw is another's individual expression of perfection. The important thing is to embrace your imperfect perfection, at any given time, and express it. The only thing that is constant is change. So, are you changing in ways that are visible in your outer life?

"Don't put off until tomorrow what you can do today."

Change happens so gradually that it is often difficult to really see the difference in your life. For me, it usually requires that I have some experience that catches me off guard. When the situation has passed and I have had time to reflect, I might notice how differently I acted or reacted. *"Wow! I really have changed. All of this work I've been doing **has** paid off."* I can celebrate my accomplishment, even if it's small, and then go on to what else I might learn from the situation. *"How could I use this experience to grow further, to emerge a different person?"*

There was a period in my life where change happened so fast that I was constantly off-center. I felt like I was shedding my skin about once a week, never totally comfortable in the one I was currently wearing. That was a really tough time. I know it had to be that way for me, because I had resisted for too long.

Given that nothing ever really stays the same, we make our lives difficult by trying to hold on to things that aren't working. Eventually the universe will cut them loose for us, if we don't do it ourselves. I would much rather be actively involved in the process so that I maintain some illusion of control. If I recognize what needs to go and take steps to make that happen, I pretty much assure myself that the transition will be a lot smoother.

The easiest way for me to explain this is to use my many years of managing people as an example. While you always hope the person that you hire loves the job and is a perfect fit, that is not always the case. More often than I'd like to admit, I've ended up with an associate that was obviously unhappy and ineffective on the job. There comes a point in time where you know that the best thing for everyone (the associate, yourself, other staff, customers) is to let the person go. Yet, if you've ever had to fire someone, you know it is one of the hardest things you'll ever have to do.

The anticipation, though, is much worse than the actual experience. You make every attempt to avoid the inevitable. If you avoid it long enough, the universe steps in and solves it for you. The impact, more often than not, is much worse. What could have been handled gently and with care turns into an abrupt natural disaster. You spend lots of energy on damage control, rather than on growing and creating.

Change happens one way or the other. We can choose to flow with it and have a gently transformational experience or resist and have the rug pulled out from under our feet. I am happy to say that the 'new me' is much better at flowing than the 'old me' would have ever dreamed of being. The 'old me' wouldn't have even understood the value in the flow. I couldn't be the 'me' I am today without having been the 'me' I was then. All the experiences I've had helped create today's version of me.

Recognizing this allows you to embrace change every step of the way... which is critical to the 'master plan'.

"Life is what you make it."

Can you accept that we all came here with a plan? Maybe not a fully-formulated plan but a broad brush of what we'd like to work on and how we want to experience life? The universe supports you in creating the situations and experiences that help you do this. You have lots of choices along the way, whether you opt for detours or the direct route.

Last year, I did a sort of vision quest with a friend of mine. It was one of the most profound experiences of my life. I saw with total clarity how we make things difficult on purpose so that we have a richer experience to work with. But this wasn't the first time I'd had this demonstrated to me.

Several years ago, I was with a group of people in Brazil, and after a gathering one evening, several of us were in a car driving back to Rio. There was a sign that pointed the direction home, but we were convinced that it couldn't be that easy since we had come a completely different and much more complicated way. After driving around for an hour, we ended up taking the route home that was initially provided to us and found our way easily.

This was another opportunity for me. I saw how clearly we chose to make things more difficult. The universe provided us with clear direction; we just weren't ready for it yet. After having the full experience, the way was made available to us again, and we were ready to take it. This is how life works.

There really is no such thing as a missed opportunity. It will present itself again. It may not be quite as readily identifiable as this example, but, on closer review, you can see how you really have been given another opportunity to choose the next level. The universe stands ready to give you whatever you desire or require. It is your higher self (the self that knows the whole plan) that is actually guiding the way.

In any situation, you can choose to take the easy road. In my case, I probably won't, but I know I can. Once you understand that and accept your responsibility in the co-creation of your life, you are powerful and inspired. You become aware of the opportunities that present themselves and see how your choices create your experiences. Every time you make a choice from total awareness and consciousness, it is a cause for celebration. It doesn't matter so much what the choice produces; it is all perfect. It is the expression of knowing yourself and what supports your personal path of self-discovery that is important.

We make lots of choices every day that we feel are pretty inconsequential. Once you begin following your own path, you'll find that every decision has consequences. *"If I am drawn to go to a certain place for lunch and choose not to go, might I miss a chance encounter that was important in my personal process?"* The opportunity will present itself again, but you have no idea what will surface during the delay. Then, there are those points when you know you're at a major crossroad in your life. If you've learned to make conscious choices with the small stuff, you can make the big decisions with much more confidence and joy.

Once you've embarked on this journey, there's really no turning back. Once you've tasted what's available to you, it is too important to ignore. You finally realize, *"There is more to life and I choose to start living it now."*

Chapter 2

Create Win/Win

"Winning is everything."

Learning to think differently is a key to getting more out of life. There are many concepts we tend to accept because they seem 'logical' on the surface. Yet, when you dig a little deeper, you find there's more to the story than you grasped with a glance.

Win/win is a perfect example. On the surface, it's a concept that seems hard to get your arms around. In real life, doesn't someone have to lose for someone to win? The problem with this is that win/lose is a short-term solution. Let's take a business arrangement for starters.

A customer negotiates the purchase price of a supplier's product down to a point where there is little or no profit. The supplier company might accept this deal because it needs cash flow in the immediate future. The customer firm thinks it really got a good deal because it saved some money, and that has immediate impact.

But look two months into the future. The supplier can't meet its cash flow demands because it had to pay the costs for fulfilling the contract. When the supplier is no longer in the channel, the customer company is forced to go into the marketplace and build a new relationship. It will ultimately have to pay a fair price for the product and will have to suffer the time-consuming process of educating a new supplier on its way of doing business.

That's why, if I have a problem with a company that's providing services to me, I feel that I owe it to them, as a fellow business owner, to talk to them about it before I make a decision to terminate the relationship. I would want the same courtesy from a customer of mine. Wouldn't you? It's much easier to fix an existing relationship than to start a new one. *And* it makes for a stronger relationship where both sides win.

Competition is really stiff in today's business world. When a company chooses to do business with you, it's important to understand that they have given you an opportunity and you should be grateful for it. The goal is to provide value beyond the services or products the customer expects.

My accounting firm's services, for example, were expensive but worth it. If a client wanted us to cut our fees or services, we would rather part company than compromise our standards. Over the years, we had many clients that left and came back. They were happy to pay us whatever it took to straighten out the mess the new accountant had made. In many cases, that was five times what they would have paid if they had stayed with us all along. While they eventually returned, knowing they would receive true value for their expense, trying to 'win' in the short-term cost them a lot in the long-run.

You can probably see how these business examples apply to all types of relationships. While you might be able to focus on winning at all costs in the near term, everyone is a loser eventually. On the other hand, if you give more than is expected, you see returns that are amazing. In our business scenario, for example, the buyer gets something of value for a price that the seller feels is fair for the services or products they are selling.

There is give and take in every relationship. In a win/win situation, both parties get as much as they give. I pay a fair price, and you get a fair profit. I give a certain amount of time, and you compensate me appropriately. You know you've created a win/win because it feels good. You can celebrate together because everyone has something to be thankful for.

Even in a sporting event, you can see win/win at work. While ultimately one team wins and the other loses, they both have an opportunity to play. The experience of just being in the game can be enough of a win to keep you coming back for more.

At first, the concept of win/win (especially in business situations) might be a little foreign. In our highly competitive world, people are programmed to beat out the competition at all costs. But if your words and actions are consistent with creating win/win, it will eventually sink in to the people you're dealing with. And once you achieve win/win, you both realize how great it feels to make a deal with someone and know that both parties are celebrating.

While I'm a Type A personality (ambitious, with lots of things going at one time), I've never been competitive. Win/lose isn't fun for me. I've learned that if you keep working on a problem, you can usually come up with a solution that is win/win.

In any negotiation, I go into it knowing where I want to end up. If getting there turns out to be a losing proposition for either party, I am willing to walk away. I know that win/lose doesn't feel good and that, even if I'm on the winning side, the benefits are short-lived. I have to accept that the only one I can make happy is myself. You have a responsibility to take care of yourself and be honest in your communication. At the end of the day, all parties will know themselves a little bit better and have a stronger relationship.

Focusing on creating a win for everyone is actually much easier than the alternative. You don't have to grind through heavy negotiations because everyone is on the same page. Together, you create something that works for everyone.

"It takes two to tango."

Let's look at an example of creating win/win in personal relationships. You are married to someone that approaches problem-solving very differently from you. While you need to confront the problem and dissect it, your spouse wants to deal with it privately and then calmly discuss what he or she has come up with.

This leaves both parties bewildered. You need to work things out together and wonder how your partner thinks a joint problem can be solved privately. Your spouse can't imagine living through the confrontation and emotional storm of working it out at the same table. In order to create win/win, both of you have to give a little. What you get in return is potentially magnificent.

Let's say you both agree you have a problem. You make a deal to give each other 48 hours to come up with several alternatives to solve the problem. At a specified time and place, you will come together and discuss your concerns, alternatives, and whatever else has come up for each of you in the process.

The most important thing to remember here is to keep the agreement. In order to build trust, you have to honor the process. In any situation, there's always the chance that the person you're dealing with will have a difficult time believing you really want to create win/win. Certainly expressing what your goal is helps. But it is really making sure your actions support what you're saying that will eventually clear the water.

So, when you come back together in 48 hours, you (as the more confrontational party) make every effort to deal with your partner as calmly as possible. Your spouse, who is more non-confrontational, works to take things less personally and to stay with the process.

This is a miraculous way to address issues. It may take some coaching the first few times you use it, but eventually problem-solving will become fun and rewarding.

Many times, you have to ask questions and feel your way through the process, because you just don't know what would create a win for the other person. The easiest way to determine if you are creating win/win is to walk a mile (or even around the block) in the other person's shoes. If you were sitting in his or her chair, would you feel like you were getting a fair deal? You have no way of knowing all the factors that influence someone else's decision-making, but you can look at things through your own version of their eyes.

Whenever I am aggravated by someone's actions, the easiest way for me to find compassion is to look for ways that I may have acted similarly. Recently, I was ready to pull out of a parking space at a grocery store. I drive a small SUV, so sometimes it's difficult to see what's behind me. I double- and triple-checked before I started backing up. Yet, somehow in the process, a girl in a little Volkswagen Bug had pulled up to the curb right behind me to drop her friend off at work. The next thing I knew I felt a bump, and I had backed into her fender.

After my initial reaction of assessing the damage, I was a little aggravated that she had pulled up without paying attention to the fact that I was backing out. There wasn't much room to work with.

It didn't take me long to have it put right back in my face. Shortly after that, I pulled up at a curb in a similar fashion and realized that someone was backing out, potentially right into me. While I'm a bit more visible in my SUV, I had done the same thing as the girl in the Volkswagen Bug had done. It happens. We don't pay full attention and inconvenience others regularly.

Next time you are mad at someone for cutting you off on the road, try moving to a time when you've been guilty of the same thing. The quicker you can do that, the quicker you will be able to get back to more productive thoughts.

"Don't overlook the forest for the trees."

Sometimes, when you are trying to get past a situation, you seem to keep bumping into yourself or obstacles that seem to be growing rather than disappearing. When that happens, it's time to step back and analyze how you are approaching the situation. If you are being presented with one obstacle after another and the universe is making things difficult, then there is something undeniably wrong with where you are going.

When you start meeting with resistance, the most logical, reliable conclusion you can come to is that there's something you don't know that is operating in the situation. A variety of ways to discover what that is will be laid out in future chapters. Right now, I just want you to trust that there is something going on that doesn't meet the eye.

A short lesson in astrology: The planet Saturn is known to professional astrologers as the crotchety old man of the universe. He is the king of limitation and responsibility, more than a little heavy. Saturn provides you with the substance that you need to really accomplish things. Without Saturn, you would be adrift.

When Saturn is influencing you, you may feel limited, like the world is working against you. More likely, you are experiencing universal adjustments that are totally necessary to get you where you say you want to go. Saturn – just like any other influence in your life – isn't negative; it's critical to your development. It is just a way to keep you on course.

Since obstacles are very clear signs from the universe that something isn't right, they are your opportunity to stop and regroup. Sometimes that means you have to abandon a plan altogether. At other times, all you need to do is alter your course slightly.

I went on a fact-finding mission last year, to see if I thought Colorado was where I wanted to live. The day I arrived, I drove up the canyon a few miles and found a piece of property that was right out of my dreams. It is a beautiful pine-covered slice of heaven, with a perfect natural building site in a meadow. I made an offer on the property and, with little negotiation, it was accepted. I have been working on a plan to build my home there, and it has pretty much fallen into place.

While building in this area is supposed to be really challenging, I haven't found that to be true in my experience. The project keeps moving forward. Every time I do encounter any resistance, it turns out to be just what I needed to alter my course slightly.

When I hit a snag, I am very clear in my intentions. *"If I am not supposed to build this house or tackle this project, I am willing to let it go."* You *have* to be willing to let it go. You can't fool the universe. It knows if you're attached to an outcome.

And if you *do* have a specific outcome in mind and are unwilling to let the universe create the best version of that for all concerned, things will get murky. Basically what you are telling the universe is that you're okay with win/lose. "I just want it my way – no matter what that takes."

Be careful! The universe will give you what you ask for. You'll end up swimming in it and wondering why you're there. On reflection, you can see how you created it. I have sometimes experienced days of anxiety in dealing with a situation, but when I finally let go, it always passes quickly and the perfect solution (I would go all the way to miraculous, in some cases) manifests. I believe that you can create whatever you want.

"Nothing ventured, nothing gained."

The clearest way to becoming a master at manifestation is to ask for whatever you desire to appear in your life, under grace in a perfect way. You have to mean it! We've all heard the stories of how someone has asked for money to manifest and it came as the result of some unfortunate circumstance, like an accident settlement. It doesn't have to be that way. You can manifest what you desire or require in a way that is for the highest good of all concerned.

I make lists and ask for very specific things to come into my life. At first, this might seem inconsistent. How can you ask for something specific and still be detached? That's where asking for 'this or something better' comes in.

You need to give the universe some idea of where you want to go and what you're ready for (or at least what you think you're ready for). When you ask for what you desire to manifest 'under grace in a perfect way', you have sent the universe clear direction. Knowing, though, that the universe is much wiser than you are, why would you want to limit yourself to what *you* can imagine? Instead, you ask for what you desire or require, ***or something better,*** to manifest in your life.

One of the reasons people limit themselves and their dreams is because we are all programmed to believe that, if we claim our 'fair share', someone else will have to go without. That is a myth and defies the laws of the universe. Universal abundance is unlimited.

When you really look at how things work, you can see that there is no correlation between what you have and what someone else has. We all create our own abundance, consistent with our belief system. If you believe the universe has more than enough to supply everyone's needs, then it will be that kind of place. It boils down to attitude.

Attitude feels like something that exists on the surface, but it really emerges from the subconscious. You have deep-seated beliefs that affect how you think and how you react to your circumstances. It takes some effort to sort through this and determine what you really believe in the light of day.

It is your destiny to have all that is yours by divine right. If you don't claim it, it will be left unclaimed. That's right! It doesn't go to someone else. It is there waiting for you.

When I sold my company several years ago, I carried a note for a sizeable balance. At the time, I asked the universe to produce a way to have the note paid off within a year. A little over a year later, through several seemingly disconnected events, I had a check in hand for the value of the note.

You never know how Spirit will take care of things. Your only real job is to ask for what you need and to trust that it will happen. You can't see into the future (at least not with the kind of clarity that the universe has at its disposal), so you need to pay attention to the signs you are given every day. The universe manifests your desires through you. In most cases, there is action required on your part. If you aren't tuned in, you won't know what the universe needs you to do.

"When 1 + 1 = 10."

It's always a challenge for companies to find qualified personnel who also fit with the firm's culture. Any new employee creates a dynamic of his own with the company he chooses to join. The company is delighted to have help. The person had all the right answers in the interview and seems like a good fit. He is excited about joining a new organization and realizing his own goals through providing his services to further the company's goals.

It doesn't take much time to know whether the association is going to work as planned. The energy created by the joining of forces is either greater than the sum of the parts or a struggle that generates stress and anxiety for all concerned. Sometimes you give more than you get, and other times it works the other way around. If someone focuses only on getting, I call that the 'You Owe Me' attitude. And you've probably run across some employees with that mentality. They were doing you a favor by showing up to work, even if they were only there physically.

How can you know with more certainty before you make the hiring decision (or accept the job) if it is going to work out for all concerned? There are always signs and feelings that will give you clear direction *if* you pay attention.

I have one instance in which I used this process that was particularly rewarding. I hired Michele about two years ago to assist with a couple of my business ventures. Our relationship has been a win/win since day one. Here's the story in her words:

"I was feeling more than a little underutilized running the local office of a computer services firm and responded to an ad for a 'metaphysical writer' in the local paper. In a flurry of e-mails and phone calls, Gala and I went back and forth about it. Several issues seemed to complicate the situation. Gala really wanted someone full-time, and I really wanted to help on a freelance basis so I wouldn't leave my current employer stranded. We agreed to put some more thought into it and touch base in a week.

A day or two later, I got a fax telling me my current employer was closing the local office. My job was going to end a week from that Friday, precisely two days before Gala had wanted me to start full-time. I called her with the news, and we both began to laugh wholeheartedly. When we finally recovered, her response to me was, "I guess it is out of our hands." I could do nothing but agree and marvel at the wisdom of the universe, as I still do. I went to work for her full-time as soon as the office closed. We have worked so well together and accomplished so much, there is no room for any doubt about how it played out. It was truly meant to be!"

And as the employer, I totally agree. When Michele first contacted me, it seemed like there were a number of logical reasons the situation wouldn't work. Yet the signs were all there to clue me into the fact that I should pursue it, so I did. Obviously, the same was true for her. We both were willing to think outside the box and strive for a win/win, and it worked.

Today, Michele has moved on from being an employee to being a valued associate. In fact, she was my 'prose engineer' for this book — the person who blended my ideas and words (much like an audio engineer mixes the music in a theatrical production) to make the experience really come together.

Another story I love, that demonstrates how important it is to pick up on the signs that are sent you, is the one about the man that was sitting on top of his house in a flood. A boat came by and offered him assistance. He said, "No, thank you. God is taking care of it." A little while later, a helicopter showed up. His response was the same. Not long after that, the waters rose and he drowned. When he got to the 'other side', he asked God why his faith had failed him. God's response was, "It didn't. I sent the boat and the helicopter." You have to pay attention and take the opportunities that have been given to you.

At the same time, you have to be willing to really turn control of the situation over to the universe. It does no good to worry. In fact, worrying is a total waste of time and extremely counter-productive. It uses valuable energy and takes you off task. Even though you know you need to be focused on picking up the universe's signals to resolve a situation, there is no way you will be paying close enough attention to take appropriate action if you're consumed with worry or fear. You probably won't even be able to get out of your own way.

Michele (my 'prose engineer') recently shared a story with me that is a great example of how trusting the universe to orchestrate things is far superior to falling prey to worry. She was supposed to report for jury duty first thing on a Monday morning (after it had been delayed multiple times for well over a month). She was also scheduled to meet with the local community college that morning to discuss doing some corporate training sessions for them.

Unsure how to resolve the dilemma, she left it up to the universe. Her jury duty got postponed from Monday morning to Tuesday at noon. While this eliminated one problem, it created another.

As an adjunct faculty member for a new college campus in town, she was due to start teaching a class on the other side of town at 6 p.m. on Tuesday. And she was not as well-prepared as she would've liked, due to some administrative mix-ups. If she were selected to sit on a jury, there was no way she could finish preparing, make the 30-plus minute drive, and still have time to grab food and set up the classroom.

When she started to stress over all this, she decided it was time to focus: *"Everything happens for a reason so I'll just 'give up' control to the universe."* A miraculous thing happened. It worked… again!

The solution went well beyond her jury duty getting postponed to Tuesday so she could make the Monday meeting. She and the other prospective jurors ended up sitting in the waiting room for over two hours, which gave her plenty of time to prepare for that night's class and even start on future weeks. When they went into the courtroom, she prayed and focused on not being selected. The court called 32 names out of 50 or so people, and hers was not one of them. None of the 32 selected were excused, so her commitment was fulfilled and she was out of there by 4 p.m., allowing plenty of time to eat and set up the class before 6 p.m. Plus, she finally had a good-sized group of great students to boot (after several cancelled classes due to low enrollment). "It was a beautiful thing," she told me.

The universe manifested the perfect solution for the highest good of everyone in the situation – Michele, the court system, the colleges, and the students. When you trust in the universe and your goal is win/win, good things happen.

"Great minds think alike."

The mind-shift to win/win is an important factor in our culture today. A new and growing segment of the population, termed 'cultural creatives' by Paul Ray, is more focused on the big picture. This group of approximately 44 million people (and growing) understands that what we do has enormous impact on our own country, the planet, and the universe. It is a much more relationship-oriented mindset.

Since, by choosing to read this book, it is highly likely you know that collaboration is much more powerful than trying to force a one-sided solution on a problem. Maybe you're also a cultural creative? How do you know? Do you take a more holistic and spiritual approach to life? Do you envision a positive future built on planetary healing, environmental consciousness, and tolerance-focused interpersonal relationships? Does your social conscience drive you to support human rights and ecological issues? Do you seek personal and spiritual growth through travel to foreign lands, activities like meditation and journal-keeping, and the use of ancient wisdom from astrology, tarot, and similar tools?

If so, then you are part of this group that wants to be all they can be and help make the world a better place. And it is this mentality that will actually make a difference, by promoting a consciousness of give and take. When you give from the heart – to your loved ones and your community, as well as any co-workers, staff, customers, and suppliers you may deal with – it comes back to you multiplied many times over. What greater win/win could any of us ask for?

Chapter 3
Metaphysical Guidance

"Mind over matter."

Do you ever wish you had all the answers? The good news is that you do. You already know everything you need to know. All the answers are available to you. It is simply a matter of connecting with the part of yourself where that knowledge lies. In essence, you're not learning, you're remembering. It's much quicker and easier that way.

I haven't ridden a bike in many years. Yet, I am confident that, if the opportunity presented itself, I could get on a bike and ride it with no preparation. The same principle can be applied to anything you undertake. So where do you start in learning to access this kind of assistance? Meditation - the most useful tool in your spiritual tool chest.

If prayer is talking to God, then meditation is a way for God to answer. Over the years, I have developed an active meditative life that, in many ways, is much more 'real' than the conscious life I lead. I have spent time cultivating relationships in meditation that have helped me through the most trying of times.

I have a guide that is always with me. Some people might liken this to having an angel present in your life. While everyone has a similar presence, it is those who take the time to connect with it that are able to see tangible benefits in their lives. Meditation gives you a way to get in touch with that 'guide'.

There are many different types of meditation, but virtually all forms take you to the same place. It is the practice, not the method, which is important. Most practitioners use one of two types of meditation:

- *Mindfulness meditation* (often referred to as Zen) - Mindfulness is the English translation of the Pali word 'Sati', which is an activity that can also be described as 'bare attention'. It embraces the fact that stress is a part of life. Mindfulness may be practiced anywhere, any time. The goal is to be able to put yourself in a meditative state while working or doing any action. This way, you can use meditation to help understand the forces in your life and find meaning in them. Once you begin to feel more confident in your ability to handle the situations that you encounter, you make better choices.

- ***Transcendental meditation (TM)*** - TM requires that you repeat a mantra for twenty minutes, twice daily, while sitting quietly in a chair with your eyes closed.

Meditation helps you maintain emotional balance and keep a sharp, focused mind so you can tune in to your intuition. In order to be an effective problem solver, you must first conquer your fear of the unknown and become comfortable in the gap between ordinary thoughts. In this space, you can develop and use your intuition to deal with issues effectively.

It is generally thought that the mind manufactures stress when it believes it doesn't have the information necessary to solve problems it detects. Meditation provides you with a centering technique that allows you to move beyond the mind's stereotypical responses and substitute creative energy for repetitive urgency. In other words, it allows you to gain perspective and control of your stress-producing mind.

When you face a stressful situation, you realize you can control your reaction to it, and it is no longer stressful. Problems become smaller as you become more centered and focused. You gain perspective more easily and see how you would like to influence the outcome of a situation, using conscious goals and plans. You grasp the problem much more quickly, and solve it much more creatively, once you understand that you need to grasp yourself first.

You can use meditation to help you purge anger, overcome prejudice, reduce tension, increase sensitivity, and resolve conflicts. In as little as three minutes, stress can be switched from 'overdrive' to 'off'. Short meditations often extend to ten or 20 minutes once you realize how good it feels to experience total relaxation. Even though you can see glimpses of the benefits of meditation very quickly, consistent long-term practice is what produces lasting transformation.

Meditation requires discipline. While it helps to be in an environment and culture that supports this practice, it is *you* who must prioritize it. The benefits far outweigh the costs. The practice of regular meditation is proven to reduce stress, improve health, create emotional stability, and, most importantly, teach you patience. If you learn nothing else, you will learn patience – a virtue most of us would like to enhance.

You will also find that meditation increases your creativity, concentration, and thinking power, allowing you to boost your personal productivity in many ways. For one, it reduces the time you lose due to anxiety and stress. Problems are resolved much more quickly so that you can get back to living life. When you practice meditation in a concentrated, disciplined way, something magickal happens.

I personally have found disciplined meditation essential to maintaining the state of mind that allows me to rise above any situation that appears difficult. Practicing meditation regularly has helped me create an automatic and positive response to anxiety as it arises, allowing me to move through it quickly and see the opportunity in whatever presents itself. It feels more natural to flow with problems in order to arrive at a solution than to force a resolution that may not be in everyone's best interest.

With all these positive results, why let another day go by? If you don't already meditate, you owe it to yourself to develop a program for incorporating this practice into your life.

"Don't forget to say your prayers."

Prayer is an integral part of meditation. Here's how I begin: *"Right now, God. I expect and claim your divine guidance and inspiration."* When you expect and claim your divine guidance and inspiration, you can be assured that the universe will make its presence known in your life. You open up a channel of communication, sort of like dialing the telephone. The more focused you are, the stronger the connection.

I am an action-oriented person. Since I always have several projects underway, I feel compelled to be highly productive in whatever I put my energy into. Early on in the process, I had a hard time seeing how meditation was going to assist me in accomplishing my goals. Sure, I might be more relaxed, but part of me thrives on the intensity. At the end of the day, I can look back and see what I've produced.

What a pleasant surprise it was to discover that my time spent in meditation was some of the most productive time in my day. The guidance I received could be put to use immediately. Before, I might have spent days trying to find the appropriate avenue to take. After a period of meditation, I can quickly choose the easiest path with confidence. Rather than spending time creating problems, I actually avoid them.

One day, I was golfing with my sister at a course we played regularly. At the time, we were both practicing CPA's and had just spent several months surviving yet another tax season. It was a beautiful May day. Sunny, light winds, and not too hot.

I had gotten divorced the year before, but I still wore my wedding ring (a stunning, three-carat, emerald-cut diamond with channel-set baguettes on either side). My former spouse and I had the ring custom-made, and it was still very special to me.

I had tried playing golf with it on my finger, but it was a bit cumbersome under my golf glove. Instead, I used to take it off and tie it in the laces of my golf shoe with a double knot. In hindsight, it doesn't seem too brilliant; but at the time, it seemed perfectly safe – and a much better option than putting it in my golf bag. In fact, it was reassuring to be able to look down and see it there on my shoe. I knew right where it was.

It was a crowded day on the course, and we were forced to play at a leisurely pace. Rather than be frustrated, we decided to just enjoy the sun and company, chatting between holes. I recall looking at my shoe at the third tee, and my ring was just where I expected it to be, perfectly secure.

On the 18th green, my sister looked at my shoe and said, "Gala! Where is your ring?" At first, I thought she was teasing me, but I soon found out that my safe, secure storage place wasn't so secure. My shoelace had come untied, and the ring was gone!

We are not great golfers and had been all over the course. If you have ever played in Las Vegas, you know that, beyond the usual hazards and expanses of a course, there are ravines and rocks everywhere. It seemed hopeless. Where would I even begin to try to find it? My sister asked me what I wanted to do and I told her I felt like we had to *try*. I needed to put forth a little effort and see if I was meant to have the ring back. Ultimately, finding a needle in a haystack is not impossible, if it's meant to be.

The ground we needed to cover was the equivalent of looking for a ring in Monet's field of haystacks. There were grass, rocks, and bushes, plus the course was home to rabbits, lizards, ducks and other animals. If one of them had picked it up, it could've ended up anywhere.

We started going back over our tracks as best we could remember. Driving into the line of fire wasn't the safest thing to do, but we needed to ask all the golfers we passed along the way if they had seen my ring. As they watched us approach, it was obvious they thought we were a couple of uneducated women playing their first round of golf. Once they heard our story, all they could do was wish us luck.

We searched back several holes, and I finally realized that it was going to take more than just *our* effort to find this ring. I sat down on the green, became very quiet, closed my eyes, and prayed, while my sister patiently waited for me.

Back then, I was not in the habit of praying, so it felt really awkward to be talking to God on the golf course. I knew I needed the help though, and who was I to say I wouldn't get an answer, no matter where I was. I really felt like God *was* listening to me.

I told God that I really wanted the ring to come back to me and that I would accept it as nothing less than a miracle if it did. If it were meant to be, I would be put in the position to find it and would never question it. I felt very connected and sat in silence for quite a while.

When I finally got up, we continued the search. We searched the green, the fairway, the ravines, and the tee boxes, trying to retrace our steps. A few more holes produced nothing. We drove up to the next tee box, and I got out to look around.

As I was walking towards the tee, something caught my eye. It was a flash in the sunlight. In the long grass, just before you step into the tee box, there was something glimmering. I walked toward it deliberately. I bent down, and there was my ring, with the diamond turned up like it was staring at me.

I picked it up with both hands and started jumping up and down, screaming, "I found it, I found it." The emotions took over and uncontrollable tears started to flow.

As we drove back to the clubhouse, everyone congratulated us. They had heard me screaming and knew I had found it. Once I calmed down, I realized the magnitude of what had happened. I had asked for help and God answered me. I claimed a miracle. I will never question it.

On that day, I felt like I really had a 'direct line'. I had entered the 'void'. There was a distinct shift in my consciousness. The key is learning how to enter that space any time you have a problem.

Since that day, I have learned to spend a good deal of time in contemplation and meditation. The benefits are enormous. Yet, even with all the guidance I feel like I receive on a daily basis, I still don't feel truly 'connected' much of the time. There are times, when I am caught up in confusion and uncertainty, that I ask God for assistance and my questions seem to return unanswered.

Whenever I start to doubt God's participation in my life, I recall the day I claimed a miracle. It was *that easy*. It was years before I fully understood the magnitude of what I had experienced. Now, I know that if I ask for what I want with clarity and purity, it will be granted.

Miracles happen every day. All you have to do is look around with intent, and you can see them everywhere. God is available to you every step of the way. My prayer was answered on the golf course. Never doubt that your miracle is just waiting to be claimed.

"Let your conscience be your guide."

Even classic children's tales, like Pinocchio, have made reference to letting the voice inside you guide you. Call it what you will — your conscience, consciousness, or higher self, it's really still about tuning in to the guidance available within you. Acting on clear guidance assures you that the results will be much better than anything you could have imagined or created on your own.

All you have to do is ask for a definitive lead, then wait. The waiting is the hardest part, but you have to let it go and move forward with attention. The lead will come, you just need to be aware of your surroundings. You may, for example, be drawn to go to a place that you wouldn't normally go. There may be a message there for you that is, in essence, the next clue in the treasure hunt. Stay tuned into your feelings – that's your intuition trying to guide you.

It really is a game, if you are willing to play. It makes it much more fun (and less frustrating) when you delight in the process. *"Where to next, Spirit?"* If you trust that you will be guided to exactly where you need to be, when you need to be there, then you will resist much less. You won't want to miss the opportunity to further yourself along in the game you're engaged in.

Trusting your guidance can be the most difficult part of the process. How do you know you're not creating an answer based on what your conscious self wants to happen? In some ways, you *are* creating the answer. The answers are within you. Meditation just helps you tap into that knowledge.

As you learn to work with your guidance, you will be able to distinguish the difference between a forced solution and something that oozes from your super-conscious mind. It isn't subtle. There is no question. When you start to follow the guidance you've received, you will find that things unfold naturally. Executing is easy.

One day, I was on the phone with an associate, discussing a project that we were involved in. There had been some miscommunication, and we needed to consult with another person to clarify several points. The person we needed to get in touch with travels extensively, and I hadn't spoken with him in several months. I had no idea if it would take two days or two weeks to track him down. I started to think that perhaps the project was becoming an energy drain and that I might be better off letting it go and focusing my energy on other things.

There are still times I wonder about (or disregard) the concepts I embrace. But it only took a moment for me to be shocked back to what is absolute reality: *"Before you ask, you have been answered."* It didn't take two days or two weeks to connect with him; it took two minutes! I didn't even have to find his phone number; he called me.

After a few minutes of discussion, I had the information we needed to move forward and realized the problems we had were actually minor. I took this as a very clear message that the project needed to move forward and that everything would be made available to me so that I would have plenty of time to meet all my commitments. And so it went.

"Let go and let God."

Sometimes you'll receive an idea or feel the need to create something new. This could prove to be a moment of truth. Most inventions are the product of divine inspiration.

You may even feel overwhelmed by a message you receive. You'll think, "How could this be true?" It helps to go into the situation and see how pure the messenger was. Did you create the vision, or was the message from someone outside of yourself? Was it confirmed?

You can always ask for confirmation. If you're not sure, don't force it. Ask to have your lead confirmed. Then wait some more.

At times, I experience meditations that leave me feeling like the curtain between the worlds opens for me. These experiences have a profound influence on my life. While I am in the middle of it, there is no question that what I am experiencing is 'real'. Yet, when I bring things into the light of day, I can't help but question, "Was that for real?"

This sounds pretty serious, but at these times, I'm usually laughing. There is no denying that I am lighter, enlightened, and emanating love.

I consider myself to be a creative person with a fairly active imagination. My imagination couldn't touch this. It is way beyond my worldly capabilities. What really amazes me is that I know what I have seen is possible. It is a version of my life I could choose to live.

That's why it's so important to follow your ideas and see where they lead you. If there is something that begs to be brought into the light, you will find the means to do it. This gets easier and more fun over time. The more you let your sense of adventure lead you, the more the universe will step in to give you direction.

I lived in Las Vegas for 29 years, the last several of which I thought seriously about leaving. I felt there was a place that was better suited to how I wanted to live my life. I explored lots of options. I thought I would end up in the Pacific Northwest, but after a couple of trips to the area, it just didn't feel like the place I would call home.

After realizing that the Pacific Northwest wasn't going to be where I would make my new home, I did some soul searching. Did I really need to move, or was I just restless?

Another short astrology lesson: The planets create energy by aspecting each other, and this energy influences your thoughts. The movement of the planets affects (or perhaps instigates) any major change in your life.

We'll go deeper into this in a later chapter. Here, I'll just emphasize that, whenever you feel compelled to make a change, you can be sure, "This too shall pass." You don't have to make the change, even if you feel like you have to do it *now*. This energy will fade away. If you are meant to let something go, in order to move on to something else, then it will happen naturally and gracefully.

Knowing all this, my urge to move was still pretty constant, and I had a list of qualifications for a new place to live. Pretty lofty goals, but I wanted myself (and the universe) to know what I was looking for. One day, I got a clear message that I needed to check out Boulder, Colorado. I had never thought of moving there before that day.

I had always liked Colorado. When I was a young girl, I would vacation there with my uncle's family. We loved hiking in the Rocky Mountains, and I have wonderful memories of those times. But any time I had thought of moving there, it was always to towns other than Boulder.

The message to check it out was confirmed a couple of times within a few days, and I decided to go to the book store and buy a travel book on Boulder to see if it 'qualified'. The more I read, the more I thought it sounded perfect. It took me a year to actually plan a trip to explore the area.

To make a long story short, the first day I arrived in Boulder, I took a look around and felt immediately at home, especially after finding my dream property. The last couple of obstacles that were preventing me from moving had fallen away in the prior months, and the timing was perfect.

A month later, I was living in Boulder and loving Colorado. It wasn't forced at all. In fact, it felt like the red carpet was rolled out for me. Every need was provided for, and all I needed to do was execute.

I believe this worked out so well because I was open to options beyond those I could consciously come up with. When affirming anything, it's important that you ask for your desires (or something better) to manifest *if* it is for the highest good of all concerned and part of the divine plan. While saying this is easy, practicing it requires fearless faith and trust.

You need to be willing to make time for self-evaluation and correction when that is what feels necessary. If what you have affirmed doesn't manifest, then you know that you have not asked for something that is part of the divine plan. Maybe you're not ready. Maybe you haven't asked in the right way. It never fails. Time reveals all. You either determine that you didn't really want what you were affirming or that the delay was extremely beneficial in some way.

You know that you are demonstrating fearless faith when you have no contingency plan. If you've asked for something to manifest and start making plans for what you will do if it doesn't, then you are actually planning for the non-manifestation. You have to genuinely turn it over and let it go. If you take time to reflect, you can see how you have (or haven't) demonstrated fearless faith.

Manifestation usually comes in the eleventh hour. Actually, more times than I'd like to admit, it occurs at 11 hours and 55 minutes. Why does it happen this way when the universe *could* manifest your desire in the blink of an eye? Because it takes that long to convince yourself that the desired outcome is probable. As the situation becomes more critical and the end nears, you get out of the way and finally trust the process.

It really doesn't have to be difficult. But it's just human nature to want to fully experience things. In order to do that, you create obstacles and polarity so that, when you reach a goal or a problem is solved, you appreciate it on a deeper level.

Have you ever set a goal that you knew would really take time and effort to reach? Not something that is on today's 'to do list', but something that would require months of diligence? When you reach the goal, the sense of accomplishment has a profound impact on your life. It builds self-esteem, and you feel inspired. You know you can accomplish anything you set out to do.

Yet, there were probably some dark moments along the way, tests or obstacles put on the path to see what you were made of. Each time you hurdled one (or used your guidance to see what purpose it was sent to serve), you knew you were one giant step closer to the finish line.

The polarity serves a purpose for a time. After all, how can you know light if you haven't experienced dark? It is up to you to choose how much darkness you need before you are completely ready for light.

When I am feeling confused or uncertain, I use my journal. It is often an awe-inspiring experience, like a conversation with God. It is virtually impossible for me to avoid seeing how I have created the situation I am facing.

Once I can see that, the alternatives appear effortlessly. I move through the issues that seemed so insurmountable moments earlier, and the energy drains from the problem, leaving me light and inspired. It is like a mind dump. You uncork the top of your head and purge all the unnecessary waste. Without all the interference, there is pure clarity.

It helps to realize that you have lived many lifetimes and accumulated knowledge that you have left buried as treasure to be discovered when you're ready. When life throws you a situation that you feel ill-prepared to deal with, given the training you've had in this lifetime, you know that you have skills far beyond what meets the eye. It's like Mary Poppins' carpet bag. You just reach in and pull out whatever you need.

"Live and learn."

With any new skill, there is a learning curve. If you can work with someone who has mastered what you're trying to learn, it can speed up the process. My only word of caution is to make sure you do not become a dysfunctional version of your teacher. You can't possibly function as them; you are an individual. You need to learn and integrate. What emerges is a new and improved version of you.

I believe the masters who have walked on this planet (and are walking among us today) are sent to show us what we're capable of. Over the years, I have taken lessons from these masters and studied with many teachers. Every one of them has added to my spiritual tool chest.

More importantly, they have helped me get to know myself better. Once I made a commitment to this path, I knew there was no turning back. I had to accept that I create my reality and am personally responsible for what does and doesn't manifest in my life. In order to apply these metaphysical principles, I have to understand what makes me tick.

The only thing that limits you is yourself and what you believe. One of the great masters, Jesus, brought this to light when he pointed out that anyone is capable of doing everything he did and more, if they only believe.

When you want to master something, you need dedication, commitment, practice, and belief. Meditation is no different. You will have periods of time when you don't feel like you're making progress, you feel like the phone line has been cut. Here, your character is being tested.

Is your subconscious attempting to sabotage your forward progress? Do you have what it takes to pursue mastery? This experience is a time of integration, a respite that is just what you need to formulate your plan for the next phase of your journey. It is persistence that will see you through.

Persistence is the difference between manifesting mediocrity and realizing your dreams. Any time you set out to accomplish something, there is a good chance you will meet with resistance.

Resistance, in terms of the obstacles you encounter on your path, is a great gift. It can show you where you need to make adjustments. It can provide you with just the juice you need to push through to the finish line. Or it can defeat you.

All of us that are living life to its full potential experience more than our fair share of resistance. We have taken on the challenge of moving a mountain and know that it will happen one rock at a time.

I am so grateful for all the assistance I receive from the universe. Any time I look at a rock and think, "I just don't know if I can lift another one," I am guided to whatever will make my task easy and successful. All I have to do is ask for help, and it's there for me. The same is true for you.

There's no time like the present to begin to manifest your dreams. The universe stands ready to be called into action.

Chapter 4

Create It In Your Mind

"Diligence is the mother of good fortune."

If you are responsible for co-creating what manifests in your life, it is important to know what you want and how you want to get there. It is up to you to create the action plan or blueprint for your path.

My most preferred time to create an action plan is at the first of the year. It is a true new beginning for me because my birthday falls a couple of days after Christmas. I spend quite a bit of time working on my plans and goals. *"What did I want to accomplish last year? What actually happened, and what didn't? Were my actions consistent with what I said I wanted to accomplish?"*

The answer to that final question is what creates your reality. If you're in Colorado and say you want to go to California but you head east, then why would it surprise you when you end up in New York? That's why you make a plan - for direction.

The first step is to determine your goals for the next year. This process can take a couple of weeks to complete to your satisfaction. Your goals need to reflect what you can truly put your heart into. You won't have much success if your goals are really things that you feel you *should* do or that other people in your life want you to focus on. Remember, your actions have to support where you say you want to go. If you say you want to be a scratch golfer, but you're not willing to spend time virtually every day at the golf course, you have set a goal that will be impossible to achieve.

Your goals should also reflect the need to have balance in your life. Certainly you will have goals for your career and relationships, but also address the areas of your life that don't get as much attention.

You want to express your goals in a way that works to convince the subconscious you are already there. Let's assume you're a few pounds heavier than you'd like to be. (Right after the holidays, that probably isn't too much of a stretch.) You write your goal, "My body is in perfect health and weighs 120 pounds. My sleek physique is maintained effortlessly."

At first, your conscious mind will go nuts. *"I don't weigh 120 pounds!* And if I did, it certainly wouldn't be maintained effortlessly." If you persist, though, your mind begins to give a little. "Well, maybe I *could* weigh 120 pounds." There are lots of examples where other people have lost weight and are healthier and happier. Logically, you can begin to see how this goal is *becoming* true. At this point, you've cleared the first hurdle.

"A picture's worth a thousand words."

To really imprint your goals in your subconscious mind, I recommend you put together a collage. You might remember making collages in school. As children, our minds spent little time rationalizing our activities. Reality was a very broad concept, and we were all about creativity. What you want is to regain that, because the creative mind is open to all possibilities.

The first time I created a collage as an adult, I had a difficult time imagining that it would be at all useful. Now it is an integral part of the process. When you are working on manifesting your goals and desires, you have to live it in your mind before it can be brought into the physical world. The collage imprints a vivid picture in your mind of what you are focusing on. Making it doesn't require thinking; it's an intuitive process designed to get the creative juices flowing.

To create your collage, you will need a few supplies. I usually buy a 24" X 36" poster board. If you are uncomfortable displaying your collage where others can see it, you may prefer to buy five pieces of 8½" X 11" poster board. There are advantages to both approaches. Using one large piece of poster board creates a vivid picture encompassing all departments of your life. The smaller pieces of poster board allow you to put them in the same binder you use for your journal, for easy reference.

You'll also need some magazines, probably about ten of them. I just save the ones I get throughout the year for this purpose so I don't have to buy new ones.

In your collage, you will want to address each department of your life – health, abundance, relationship, career. Then, the center of the large collage (or the fifth piece if you're using 8½" X 11" boards) will support the general direction of your life. What would your life look like if your desires had been manifested in the physical world?

To get the images I need for my collage, I usually flip quickly through the magazines, pulling out pages that catch my attention. It could be a word, a phrase, an image, or any other message that strikes me. When you see something interesting, pull out the whole page and set it aside. Remember, this is about developing your intuition. Thinking isn't necessary. Your potential is tapped through the creative process.

Once you feel complete and have pulled out what you think you need, trim out the picture, word, or phrase that you want to use to imprint the vision. Then, start placing the items on the poster board. Once you have all the images laid out, glue them down. (I discovered the glue stick this year, and it made my life much easier.)

Making my board for this year was an incredible experience. I started it several weeks before I had time to complete it. I was a bit concerned that it might lose something with time. Boy, was I wrong! It all fell into place and created the vision with clarity and amazing detail. When it was all done, I knew there was one thing missing. I picked up a magazine that I hadn't looked at before and flipped the page to the perfect image. It was the piece that synthesized everything. I couldn't think of anything else to say but, "Thank you, Spirit."

"One good turn deserves another."

I've grown to expect this sort of guidance, and I know that it is my daily practice that helps me maintain this focus. You wouldn't think about going a day without brushing your teeth, and spiritual grounding is an equally important task. There will be days when you feel you don't have enough time to spend an hour meditating or writing in your journal, so find what works for you. Develop a practice that can be completed in 15 minutes that includes a short centering exercise and daily affirmations that support your goals.

Affirmations are different from goals. They are more personal. In my example of wanting to become a scratch golfer, I indicated that it would require daily practice. If you are finding it difficult to practice daily, you need to figure out what you need to change about yourself to make it easier to practice or keep your commitments. You might affirm that you have plenty of time to accomplish everything you have set out to do. If it's a commitment issue, then the affirmation would center around keeping commitments and following through.

With affirmations, it is more about who you are than what you do. Nothing changes until you change. As you alter your own behaviors, you become a magnet for what you want to attract into your life. Some of the personal affirmations I use include: *"I attract like-minded companions everywhere I go." "I am charming and loving in every encounter." "I have mastery-level knowledge for everything I undertake."* Taking a closer look, you can see how these affirmations are not asking for something to manifest. They are instead about how you want to be in the world.

So, now that you know where you want to go and how you want to be, the question becomes one of how you are going to get there. A written plan is a well-accepted method of getting from point A to point B. This method is used with total commitment in business environments. The action plan is more than just your goals in writing. It's a full-blown plan with the steps necessary to get you where you say you want to go. You want your plan to be a stretch but not unrealistic.

Everyone approaches tasks differently. By now, you know yourself well enough to know what you need to do to tackle the steps necessary to accomplish your goals. No step is too small.

Your action plan starts out with things you need to do this month, usually related to each goal. Then you make a three-month and a six-month plan. Don't spend a lot of time on the longer-term plans, because you know there will be lots of forks in the road over the next several months. There's no use putting that much energy into something that will no doubt change dramatically.

Once you've written your plan, look at it frequently. It isn't the kind of thing you stick in a drawer and forget about. I keep mine with my journal and, since I spend a lot of time there, it is a natural way to keep me focused. It is important to regularly spend some time truly evaluating what you've accomplished.

I like to check my progress on the current month's plan at the new moon. This is also a great time to create your new month's action plan. Since I make it a point to celebrate the change of seasons, I sit down with the whole plan at the solstices and equinoxes — great times for evaluating what you've done in the last few months.

Take time to pat yourself on the back for the risks you take along the way. With every step, you had to confront a fear, feel it, and then take the necessary step anyway. That's to be congratulated. Fear is the thing that keeps us all trapped in mediocrity. When you move through your fear, you are truly triumphant.

"No risk, no reward."

Once you start using this method of creating your life the way you'd like it to be, you're sure to encounter times of confusion and uncertainty. As you start to create your life differently and the universe starts to work with you, amazing things will manifest. Along with that, your subconscious will begin to feel threatened.

The tricky thing with the subconscious is that you can think you have an idea of what you're dealing with, but it really is elusive. It weaves and dodges. It's pretty invested in the programming it is running on. As you implement your plan, your subconscious starts to recognize that what you are affirming really could happen.

One of the sayings I use to help me understand the craziness in the world is, "Desperate people do stupid things." I think this can also be applied to the subconscious. Although it will benefit every part of you to let go of the old, dysfunctional programming that is messing with your life, your subconscious (just like lots of other affected parties) isn't sure it's willing to let go of the known for the unknown.

It's sort of like the game show, Let's Make a Deal. You know there is a better than average chance that what you are moving towards is much better than what you have now. But what if it isn't? What if you've traded your old, dysfunctional, familiarly-comfortable life for the clunker behind 'Door Number Three'? The biggest risk you have is that you will sabotage your progress unwittingly.

Your subconscious can be a formidable opponent. It has a highly-evolved defense mechanism and will attempt to preserve the status quo. If you try to meet the foe head on, you will be up against enormous resistance. Rather than beating down the front door, look for a window that is ajar. Little by little, the subconscious will release its programming.

A child doesn't learn to walk overnight. It is a long process of rolling over, crawling, pulling itself up, standing, and finally taking that first wobbly step. You wouldn't be surprised if you stood your baby up on its legs and it fell over when you let go. The same will happen if you don't coach your subconscious through the releasing of your old, limited beliefs.

Do you ever get just what you ask for (or even more) and then sabotage it? It disappears before you even have time to enjoy it. More than likely, this happens because you haven't prepared your subconscious for something that wonderful.

Part of the preparation process is dreaming of the outcome you want to manifest. You create it in your mind in living color. What does your life look like once you have claimed what you are setting your sights on? The more you live it in your subconscious, the more comfortable it will feel when it manifests in the physical world.

My niece got a new bike for her last birthday. It was a 'grown-up bike' without training wheels, and it scared her at first. The new bike sat in the garage for many months while she continued to ride her old, smaller one with the training wheels. Eventually, she 'grew into' it. It wasn't about her physical size (that didn't change much in a few months); it was her confidence level. She needed to *see* herself riding the new bike. Now, she rides it with ease and grace. In fact, she makes it look effortless.

No risk, no reward. When you take a small step in the direction that presents itself, you begin to chip away at the subconscious blocks to manifesting your desires. And by the time you get to that point, it won't even feel like an option to stay with the familiar. Once you stick your toe in the water and realize it isn't going to suck you in, the possibilities are too tempting to just sit on the fence.

When you see yourself doing or having something, it can happen in a flash. The subconscious works with you, rather than against you, in creating what has been imprinted on its screen. It really can be easy. The universe is there to support you. All you need to do is move in your chosen direction.

I was returning from a business trip a couple of years ago and had to change planes in Phoenix. It was Saturday evening, and I just wanted to be home. My scheduled layover was two hours. Surely, there was a better option.

The airlines had an earlier flight, but it took off five minutes after my scheduled arrival, and it departed from a different concourse. A five-minute window of time hardly seemed sufficient, but I was motivated. It was also a good test. Could I really walk my talk? I knew that I had to *see* myself getting off the plane in Las Vegas at 9:05, the time of the earlier arrival. There is a digital clock in the Las Vegas airport that I held in my mind reading 9:05.

When I got off the plane in Phoenix, one of the flight attendants called the flight I was attempting to make to tell them I was on my way. They were standing there waiting for me. The plane was ready to push back. They told me they didn't have a seat assignment for me and I said, "It's OK, I'll sit anywhere."

When I got off the plane in Las Vegas, there it was, the clock that had helped me create an environment of expectancy. I knew it would be 9:05 when I got home. The reasoning mind would have never allowed me to make that plane. It took fearless faith and focused intent.

"No pain, no gain."

This doesn't mean there won't be challenges along the way. One of the ways you can be tested is by experiencing an extended period of time during which, for all intents and purposes, nothing happens. This leaves you bewildered. *"I've done everything I know to do. I've been paying attention. Why hasn't it worked?"* We've discussed this before, but I can't remind you enough. This is a sign that something isn't quite right. You are asking for something that isn't in your best interest, or the universe is busy reorganizing things to actually make it happen.

Spend some time re-evaluating. Are you sure that what you've asked for is really what you want? Spending time in meditation will usually produce the missing link. There will be some obvious adjustment that you need to make.

Another challenge you may face is having something happen to you that isn't exactly what you had hoped; it might, in reality, even be classified as something you would have avoided at all (if not most) costs, given a choice. If you're like me, you're asking, *"Why do 'bad' things happen?"*

On pondering the situation, you'll probably realize that your thoughts created it.

Maybe you'll even be willing to admit that you asked for it. It may have to do with what are you working with in this lifetime. If you're stuck working with the same thing over and over, sometimes you need a jolt to move forward.

It reminds me of my computer programming class in college. If you didn't give the computer just the correct set of variables or word something exactly right, it would take off in a loop that was unrecoverable. The only way to get out of it was to press CNTL ALT DEL and reboot.

That's what the universe does. It reboots you sometimes. The pain caused by this is directly proportionate to how stuck you are in the patterns of your past.

Another way you can get sidetracked is by taking a small demonstration of what you've asked for as the universe's final answer. Let's say you've asked for financial assistance. You need $1,000 for some obligation. After doing your 'work', the universe clearly has answered with $100 from some unexpected source.

This is what could be called a 'sign of land'. The universe is moving things for you, but now is the time for you to shift into high gear, applying more focus and intent. *"I will not accept less – only more."* That doesn't mean you're not grateful for what you have received, only that you know your manifestation is not complete. If anything, this is a clear sign that you're well on your way.

"All in divine time."

What do you do when you run into a situation where what you ask for doesn't manifest? I had studied metaphysical concepts for years. I believed that the universe provides what you need when you need it. I had experimented with *"Ask for what you want, and you will get it,"* only to be disappointed when it didn't always work.

Deepak Chopra would explain this through his concept of detachment. It's a matter of being attached to, rather than detached from, a specific outcome. While in concept this is true, it doesn't help with your immediate concern. You want something you aren't receiving. It isn't supposed to work that way. You begin to wonder. "Now why didn't it manifest? Are all these metaphysical concepts for the birds? Do we really get what we ask for?"

If we profess to understand the concept of 'divine time', then why are we so impatient? For over two years, I needed a new tenant for a building I own. I couldn't understand why this wasn't manifesting, when other desires I had were falling into place. For the longest time, it seemed unrelated to the fact that I had a partner in owning the building who also shared my business. Over time, things became clearer.

I had been discontented with my work for years and finally told my partner that I was ready to sell my shares to him, if he wanted to buy them. We finalized the deal within a couple of months and proceeded with the transition. During this time, I continued to work on manifesting the new tenant. It really appeared that it would be in everyone's best interest.

As the transition year progressed, we started looking towards the one-year anniversary and a big payment that was due me. The plan was to take a portion of the equity out of the proceeds from refinancing the building to make the payment to me. The bank wouldn't refinance the building without the space being leased, and it appeared that the only way to settle the matter was to work out an arrangement where I would receive the building for the balance due on my note.

It was a risky proposition for me since I had no cash flow and the building was a drain. I trusted universal supply, and it paid off. My intuition told me that I needed to get the paperwork taken care of before the building could be stabilized. Within a week of signing all the paperwork, I got a phone call that changed everything.

A woman, who was looking to move her offices in order to take on some larger accounts, came by to look at the space. Within a couple of weeks, I had signed leases for the space. The tenants were in and enjoying their new business home a few weeks later. This cleared the way for the loan, and things changed dramatically, virtually overnight.

Logic would have said that I needed a leasing agent, negotiations would take months, and the tenants would be planning six months in advance. But logic doesn't work when you turn things over to Spirit. Spirit knows no time. Now is as good a time as any.

What Spirit does know is what is in your best interest. That's why you ask for something to manifest *only* if it is for the highest good of all concerned. In my case, it was best for both my partner and I to settle the note this way. Both of us were able to move forward on creating our vision and leave the past behind us.

Whenever I wonder what could possibly be in the way of manifesting something that I truly desire, I draw on experiences like this one. There is no rushing divine time. Impatience only brings about unpleasant experiences. While I might have been able to force things to happen by making a bad deal, forcing things is never the best way to go in the long run. I don't even consider it an option now.

I'll never forget the morning I finally understood how the process of selective manifestation works. I was reflecting on the prior day in my journal. I had run into someone I hadn't seen in a very long time. The encounter was a direct answer to what I had asked for the day before.

This struck me as fascinating. Why was this request being answered while so many others went unanswered? The conclusion I came to is that I asked the right question at the right time. Or more accurately, I asked for something I was ready for. That day, it all became clear.

If you are asking for something that doesn't seem to be manifesting in your life, ask yourself a couple of questions. *"How might I **not** be ready for what I'm asking for? How might I be stuck in something that is limiting me?"* Be patient (easier written than done). The answer comes when you are prepared to hear it.

You really are divinely guided and protected. When you ask for something, the universe takes a look at your motivation and what you're working with. When you're really 'ready', it happens, even instantaneously if your belief system allows that.

"Where there's a will, there's a way."

The thing that perplexes me more than anything about this process is how some things manifest within moments and others seem to elude us forever. I've noticed that when I ask for something that doesn't require anyone else's energy, it manifests very quickly. It's just about me and the universe, not much juggling required. When I ask for something that is more complicated, it seems to take longer.

It's times like these when your commitment is tested. Is this really something you're willing to be persistent about? Do you continue to focus intently on the outcome? If you look at your goals after a period of time, you'll find that some things just don't seem too important anymore. You might find that there's just not enough energy to go around.

Life tends to dilute you. We all complain that there isn't enough time to do everything we would like to do. By the time you have completed all the little tasks that are required of you every day, you could just accept that there is no time left to persist towards your goals. Don't buy into this! All it takes is a bit of intentional prioritization to see how you actually create things to do that keep you from the job at hand.

The goals you apply consistent, persistent energy to are the ones that eventually work themselves out into conscious reality. You know from experience that anything can manifest and miracles do happen. You can get to wherever you want to go. There is plenty of time for everything. The questions to ask yourself are how much you're willing to commit to get there and if you will want it when you get it.

Persistence is the difference between seeing lukewarm results and reaching the pot of gold at the end of the rainbow. There are so many examples from the lives of famous people that you can use to help yourself hold the vision. When you hear the story of how someone achieved success against all odds, you can use that to remind yourself that the universe can do for you what it has done for others.

Remember, though, the universe can only do *for* you what it can do *through* you. It can only create for you what you can imagine. You have to work at it. There will no doubt be many forks in the road on the way there. It will be up to you to stay tuned in enough to know which direction to go. The signs will be there. You just have to pay attention.

Learn to make good use of the time the universe gives you when you're waiting for something to manifest. Rather than sitting around thinking about what you would like to happen, take a look at your action plan and get to work. Undoubtedly, there is something constructive you could do to further yourself along in the process.

I'm not necessarily talking about taking action that would directly create the desired result, unless you have received a really clear indication that it is time to move forward. The action I'm talking about demonstrates detachment. You trust the universe and are willing to move on to another goal in the interim. If you can't come up with something constructive to do after looking at your action plan, do things you might not normally do, something fun and inspiring. Live and let live.

When you really let it go and trust that Spirit is taking care of it, you can enjoy the moment. It's so much easier to stand aside and let infinite intelligence make your way easy and successful, instead of trying to force things. What you desire will manifest when the time is right - and not a moment sooner!

Chapter 5

Thoughts Create Reality

"Look on the bright side."

There is a great deal of scientific support for the concept that your thoughts actually define you. If you think a situation is a problem, it will, in fact, be a problem. How many times have you had something 'bad' happen to you and responded with a comment like, "That's just my luck?" It's no wonder that the universe continually sends you similar situations. You've basically told it that's what you expect.

A more constructive approach is to take some time and retrace your steps. What have you thought or said that might have created this situation? The universe has no sense of humor; it takes things quite literally. Whatever you continually affirm, you will manifest.

You won't have to experience this too many times. When you see yourself clearly in the mirror and aren't happy with what is reflected, then it's easy to change. It's almost self-preservation at that point. The beauty of the process is that you can reverse it overnight. Once you realize where you have strayed, you can start planting the seeds for what you want and experience a magnificent shift.

Meditation will help you begin the process of observing your thoughts. Thoughts happen so quickly that it is nearly impossible to dramatically change what you think without processing why you think that way. As your skill builds, you will take this process into your day and start to see how unacceptable thoughts slip through your filter. When you understand the 'why', then you can begin the reprogramming process.

Let's say you're late for work. You know you have to cross the railroad tracks, and while you're hoping that you will miss the train, your mind releases the thought that a train will come by just in time to delay you further. If you're not in the habit of observing your thoughts, this goes by unnoticed. When you pay more attention, you can see how you have contributed to the possibility that you will be forced to wait for the train.

The first step in recovery is to cancel the thought and replace it with what you really want. "*Cancel that!* The universe is cooperating with me and making my commute to work quick and easy." Still, on some level, you might need the train. Maybe you haven't yet processed and released the reason you're running late. Perhaps there's something going on at work today that is making you anxious. Stopping for a few minutes (thanks to the train) can give you just what you need to adjust your attitude before actually getting to work.

Another way you attract negativity into your life is by judging others. Let's say you are one of those people who insists that your handbag matches your shoes. You are walking across a parking lot and notice that the woman you just passed obviously doesn't realize how important this is. You might have made a comment to yourself, "Isn't that tacky? A brown handbag would have been much more appropriate."

Most of us would feel this is harmless. But this ridiculous example points out that judgment, no matter what your intention, is judgment nonetheless. When you start holding others up to your standards, where do you stop? When you pass homeless people on the street corner, what is your first thought? Do you feel sorry for them? Do you condemn them for not having a job?

Either way, you've judged them by your standards. You have no way of knowing what brought them to that place. You also can't possibly know what path their soul is on. They are exactly where they need to be. My initial thought when I see someone in that position is one of wonder. What brought them to that place, and why are they there? In some way, they have chosen that path.

You can choose to help them, if that feels right for you. But look at why are you helping. Try to recognize where you are coming from, in terms of passing judgment on their situation.

"Take the road less traveled."

Thoughts are a great way of seeing how you've grown. If you always used to think how awful homeless people's lives must be when you passed them on the street, and today you just wondered what brought them to that place and how they felt about being there, you can see how things have shifted. It's working!

Sometimes my thought process really surprises me. Someone called me the other night and told me that he wouldn't be able to meet a deadline that we had agreed to. This potentially set a project we had been working on back at least a week, and the pressure increased with every delay. I thought about it for a moment and determined that this delay must serve a purpose. I had watched the universe create perfection from situations like this too many times to doubt it now.

What amazed me, though, was that the 'new me' turned over full control of the situation. The 'old me' would have complained or assumed that this would have a negative impact on our project. Rather, I immediately assumed it was part of the 'plan'. The delay was perfect, and I didn't have to know why right now. I just had to trust it.

A few days later, it became clear. On reviewing the documents related to the project, we had overlooked a significant requirement. If we had moved forward on the initial time schedule, we might easily have experienced a delay of a month instead of a week. The new 'discovery' allowed us to recreate a part of the project, and the results were far superior to what was being replaced.

There are moments in your life that are turning points, when you see clearly how to best use your time and efforts, like the 'new me' did in dealing with the week delay. The challenge is to recognize when you're at a fork, or better yet a 'T', in the road. You can continue going straight, doing the same thing you've done for years (getting the same results), or you can make the turn. Depending on the magnitude of the decision, that turn can be pretty scary.

If you slow down and evaluate all your options *before* you make the turn, you'll minimize the discomfort. Sometimes you might even need to come to a full stop to increase your comfort level. If, on the other hand, you careen out of control around the corner *then* jerk to a stop to evaluate what you've done, you'll likely encounter a lot more resistance.

I'll give you an example. For several years, I had been unfulfilled in my work. While I loved many aspects of it, I knew that I was supposed to be doing something very different. The thought of giving up my successful company, that I had spent most of my waking hours nurturing over the past 15 years, petrified me. I was sure I was just going through a phase and that my discontent would pass. That didn't happen, and I eventually let it go. If I wasn't fully committed to the company, I had no business being there.

This wasn't a hasty decision. I evaluated all my options. I prepared myself, the company, and anyone else I anticipated would be affected for the transition. Consequently, I have never had a moment's doubt since I left that I did the right thing for everyone. Had I not taken the time to really look at the situation *before* I acted, I'm sure things would have turned out much differently.

When you have a new idea or thought that is inspiring or demands attention, make time to develop it. Slow way down, put on your turn signal, and look around. *"If I take this turn, what is going to happen? If I don't take it, will I miss an opportunity that may not present itself again for a long time?"*

The new idea generates its own energy, so you'll want to capture the idea and incorporate your new learning into your plan and goals. (If you don't do that, there is a good chance you will lose much of your direction.) Then, make a point of using the idea's energy to help you take advantage of the universe's help in moving things forward.

"It's written in the stars."

Astrology is a fascinating study that can help you better understand your thought processes. I learned this from my dad, who is a professional astrologer. For any of you who live in that world, he is a licensed hermitician and certified by the American Federation of Astrologers. Long ago, he began studying astrology to help him pick the winning team in baseball games, but he got much more than he bargained for. It has become a way of life for him, with the baseball game analysis long left behind as insignificant.

My dad and I love to talk philosophically about how the universe works. One morning I called him, because I woke up with the burning desire to know what came first, the chicken or the egg. An answer came to me in a flash. It was the *thought* of an egg.

Nothing comes into reality without first becoming a thought in the universe. This was the first astrology lesson my dad helped me learn. It happened when I was 16 years old.

I had just gotten a brand new Chevrolet Monza. We had ordered it from a dealership, and it was exactly what I wanted. My dad matched the money I had saved so that I had a nice down payment, but I had to pay all the expenses of driving the car.

My sister was a couple of years younger than me, and I would take her to middle school on my way to high school. As we were crossing a major intersection a few minutes from the house, we were struck from the side by a car I didn't see coming. At 16 years old, I was ill-prepared to deal with a situation like this. I was sure that, in some way, it was the other guy's fault. I didn't believe for a moment that I could have created this myself. So, my dad gave me a lecture on the metaphysician's approach to defensive driving.

In astrology, the planets are big masses of energy. As the planets move through space, they align with each other in certain ways and create a combination of energy that acts like a trigger. Each planet's energy has a certain emphasis in your life.

While this energy doesn't really make you act on something, it does start the thought process. Through conscious choice, you can choose to do whatever you want to with the thoughts (i.e., energy). First, you have to be able to observe and capture them. This is what I lacked at the age of 16.

Once I learned about these astrological influences, I realized I had thoughts that made the environment ripe for my accident. I was responsible. Since then, the universe has helped me produce a few more accidents that technically were not my fault. Either I wasn't behind the wheel or the officer at the accident scene cited the other driver. I needed these situations to realize that I was the only common denominator. My thoughts *were* having an impact. A tremendous gift became available to me, once I fully understood how the planets helped that happen.

My theory is that God created the planetary system to avoid having to micromanage the universe. The planets move with precision and reliably create the energy for the thoughts that ultimately keep you on track (or at least on the track you originally said you wanted to take). As you become more masterful at observing your thoughts, you become more intentional in creating your life.

Throughout your life, you are given windows of time where energy is ripe to create something different. When you are aware of this energy, you can work in cooperation with it. In essence, you co-create with the universe and use the energy to your advantage.

One of the universe's most important timing aspects relates to the moon's movement. In astrology, there are 12 houses (or departments) of life. The progressed moon travels through each house over a 30-year period, taking approximately 2½ years to travel through one house. In your personal life, you can attribute a 'phase' you are going through to the location of the progressed moon. It is amazing to watch my thoughts change as the moon progresses.

In my case, the moon is currently crossing into the 7th house, the department of partnerships. Several years ago, after selling my share of the accounting business, I wouldn't have thought about going into another partnership. As far as I was concerned, I had already had the best business partner I could have hoped for and felt no need to test the waters again.

Recently, my thoughts have begun to shift. Partnership feels appealing to me now. There is no question that I will attract a partner into my life as a result of my thoughts. As I attract potential partners, there is a good chance that I will have to filter through several options before finding the 'right one'. The partner energy will want me to just get a partner. I need to make sure that I'm prepared and that my selection adds to both of our lives.

Whenever you're feeling the need to make a change *right NOW*, ask yourself if you could be going through a phase. How long have you been feeling like this? Have you asked for guidance and felt led to whatever is next for you? It is this understanding that will help you make good use of the energy, rather than become a victim of it.

If it's meant to be, it won't go away. Haste makes waste. Small movements in the new direction will inevitably show you if you have the universe's support. Your way will be made easy and successful, like following clues in the cosmic treasure hunt.

When you realize there are levels beyond your conscious reality that are much more powerful than you are, you can start working in cooperation with them and avoid a long, unpleasant journey. The principle is like that behind psychotherapy: if you can see how you deal with certain situations you're confronted with, they no longer have power over you. You can, from that moment forward, choose to do things differently.

The first step is to become aware that you have a problem. Then you move to understanding. Finally, the understanding allows you to take action, ultimately producing different results. This process can take a few moments or a lifetime, depending on how open you are to moving through it.

When I was in counseling after I got divorced, I would spend an hour discussing my reaction to situations in my life. As I left the office, I felt totally prepared to act and react differently. It was draining to watch myself make the same errors, time after time. I knew that I needed to do it differently, but somehow I would get caught up in the moment and fail miserably.

I went through this demeaning process for six months before I was forced to admit that there was something working through me that wasn't a conscious choice. I had to get to that place and convince the 'driver' that we wanted to go in a different direction. That was the moment of truth when I knew I needed to learn how to work with the powers beyond my conscious reality.

"Faith will move mountains."

Change *can* happen gently if you don't resist too much. How do you really feel about change? It probably depends on what it is. If you're five pounds lighter or you just won the lottery, it's great. If you lost a key employee, found out you have a new manager, or broke your arm, it's not so great. That's about as honest as anyone can be. The circumstances color everything.

How can someone say, "I don't like change?" Since inherently you always want to improve something, you are always asking for change, even if it's just shifting out of your comfort zone. Sometimes it's a welcome shift, and sometimes it takes some work to make it palatable.

The key to embracing every situation is reminding yourself, in the moment, that nothing is all good or all bad. Any time you label a situation 'bad', you are condemning it when you don't even know what is in store.

I had purchased an older home several years ago and was in the throws of an extensive remodel. Well into the process, it was discovered that the drain in the second bath was completely obstructed. I hadn't planned on making any changes there, so it certainly seemed like 'bad news'.

My plumber came out and tried to clear it. I had worked with him for several years, and he had gotten me through some challenging plumbing problems before. When he told me it was hopeless, I was tempted to trust him. His suggestion was to tear the whole shower out and basically build the bathroom from scratch. After he left, I meditated on the problem. "Spirit, I don't see a need to put resources into this bathroom, so I would appreciate your help clearing this drain."

My next call was to the drain experts. I told the dispatcher my whole story, and she said she would send her best man. He had a history of working through the most difficult obstructions. He showed up a short time later and went to work. After a couple of hours, he had made virtually no progress. Even from the 'drain expert', it was hopeless.

I still couldn't see any reason why I needed to remodel the bathroom. It wasn't used very often. Tearing everything up and changing it seemed like a total waste of resources. So, it was back to meditation. *"Spirit, I **know** you can solve this problem. There is nothing I can do; it is up to you."*

I called a third company out to tackle the problem. This time I didn't tell them anything beyond that the drain was clogged. When the man arrived, I showed him where the work needed to be done and told him I needed to run a couple of errands and would be back shortly. I knew I needed to detach from the situation and trust that the problem would be solved. As I ran my errands, I prayed. I envisioned the man being successful in his job and myself ecstatic at the good news I was receiving when I returned home.

I was gone about a half hour, and when I got back, he was packing up. I said, "How did it go?" His response was, "No problem. It's all taken care of." I'm sure he had never seen such jubilation from a customer before. I thanked him and shared with him how he was the third person I'd had out to try to clear the drain. After he left, I sat in awe at how things worked out.

My persistence paid off in more ways than one. Not only did I avoid remodeling that bathroom, but I took an amazing leap forward in my confidence. I had been willing to do what I needed to do to claim my miracle, if that's what it would take to clear the drain, and it worked. In refusing to believe what I was told, I reaffirmed that the universe really does hear my requests and work with me.

There is no room for doubt, which is far different from detachment. When you doubt that a problem *will* be solved, you start making contingency plans. When you detach from the problem, you know it *can* be solved and you're willing to allow the universe to solve it in whatever way is most appropriate.

"Waste not, want not."

Once you experience your own miraculous solution, there will be no turning back. You will know, like I do, that *any* problem can be solved if you're willing to think your way through it. If you've got a stubborn situation that just isn't going away, you will know that you haven't spent enough time analyzing it for its value.

One of the easiest ways to detach from a situation and lift any anxiety you're feeling is to ask, *"What's the worst thing that can happen?"* Asking yourself this simple question brings things back into perspective. You realize it just isn't that big of a deal, instead of building things up to monumental proportions and feeling like the world is coming to an end. You know you've met the dragon many times before and survived; in fact, you've emerged a hero. This time will be no different.

It is so much easier to ask the universe for help than to imitate the bull in the china closet. You will have a sense of peace about the situation when you have done all you know to do. It's out of your hands, and your job is to get back to the next task that needs your attention.

This requires focused intention. With the bathroom drain, I had to persist through several 'experts' telling me that I just needed to accept the fact that I was going to have to tear the whole bathroom apart. At the time, there was no one I could talk to that would have understood my method of solving the problem. It was between me and God.

I had been shown enough times and in many ways that anything is possible. Was I willing to insist that this was one of those times where I would demonstrate that? The miracle was there to be claimed. It simply required that I get serious about attracting it into my life at that time.

The more I use this alternate approach to solving problems, the more comfortable I get with it. While I don't mind confrontation when I feel it's necessary, I have come to enjoy using this fairly passive way (by most people's standards) of approaching a problem.

The more time you spend studying and applying these principles, the more second nature they become. While I still admit to having moments of distress when I encounter a problem, I move virtually instantaneously into the opportunity that is presenting itself.

Every situation is an opportunity to get to know yourself a little better. *"What works for me? What do I need to do to shift my energy and perspective to make way for the miracle?"* You won't have time to play the victim who thinks things happen *to* you. You will want to get on with it and put the situation behind you. As a sage, you know that you create all events and that the universe's army is with you in every battle.

Chapter 6

Know You Don't Know

"To err is human."

If you are locked inside a closed mind, you produce the same results again and again, even when the cast of characters and the scene is very different. By approaching a problem with a closed mind, you limit the limitless potential of the universe. Instead, you want to give the universe every opportunity to create the most beautiful outcome imaginable for you. When you know you don't know the perfect outcome, your mind is open to all possibilities.

When I was in my twenties, I thought I really knew what I wanted. I had my own successful business. I was married to a successful, intelligent man. We had the resources to travel and do what I thought was experiencing life to its fullest. Occasionally, I will stumble across an issue that triggers a remnant from that period. My priorities, thought process, and approach are so different now that I don't think I would recognize the person I was then if I hadn't lived in her body.

My ego would be shattered at all the seeming mistakes I made back then if I didn't have an open mind and the ability to accept that I experience profound change as I learn and grow. When you approach life with an open mind, being a humble person is pretty much guaranteed. Humility is a great character trait. It is wonderful to be wrong and be willing to admit it.

After letting go of my business, I had time to do things that I had wanted to do for years. Since the day I read my first Richard Bach novel, I knew one day I would learn to fly. For a fellow freedom-seeker, this was alchemy.

A good friend of mine is also interested in aviation, so I asked him where I should take lessons. Within a week, I had my flight bag and was standing next to the plane I would get my pilot's license in – a Piper Warrior. My instructor was great. He was a handsome, well-built guy with a sarcastic sense of humor. He had trained at Flight Safety and was no nonsense when it came to procedure, but he still knew how to make it fun.

I'll never forget my first day on the radio. We took a short cross-country trip to a nearby airport. I was supposed to practice calling all my turns over the radio, in the pattern (crosswind, downwind, base, approach), and then finish with a touch and go. In the world of aviation, the pattern is the rectangle that the plane makes around the runway as it prepares to land. A touch and go is a landing with an immediate take-off.

There was another plane in the pattern that day, and I was struggling to keep the proper distance from the other plane, maintain altitude, prepare for landing, and call every turn. I had never felt that overwhelmed in my entire life. Small planes seem to move pretty slow compared to the big jets, but when the runway is approaching at 80 miles per hour, it is plenty fast for me.

I maintained my composure until we got back to our home airport. As my instructor and I went over the flight, I couldn't keep it together any longer. I lost it and started sobbing. He looked at me and asked, "Are you OK?" Between sobs I said, "No!" He told me I had done really well at maintaining my composure; he had no idea I was on the edge of a breakdown.

After that day, I knew I would make it. Flying was the most challenging thing I had ever tackled, and I was ready.

It was almost a year later when I finally took my solo cross-country trip. Most student pilots plan a trip to remote areas so that they won't have to deal with traffic and a tower. I was just the opposite. I wanted to see what I was capable of.

It was winter, so several places were off-limits because the weather would be too unpredictable. I finally settled on Palm Springs. The manager of the flying club I rented the plane from said it would be good experience. The Palm Springs airport manages lots of traffic, including commercial jets.

The day came to take the trip, and I had done my homework. I felt well-prepared and confident. While some pilots don't make use of it, I opted for flight following (a service that is provided to all planes, on request, where you are tracked on radar and stay in constant communication with a live person). I find it comforting to know that someone knows right where I am when I fly.

As I approached Palm Springs, flight following turned me over to the Palm Springs tower, and I began my initial approach in preparation for landing. From 1,000 feet in the air, the airport can be very confusing. Fortunately, I could see the extra-large, well-marked runway just ahead and started executing my landing procedure.

There was a small plane behind me, and I heard him call the tower. "Palm Springs tower, Cherokee 1-7-5-3 Juliette. The plane ahead of me is really low. Tell her to pull up. She's really low." I wondered what he was talking about. I am always the pilot that is too high. I liked the extra room, just in case I wanted to abort the landing.

"Warrior 1-4-7-4 X-ray, Palm Springs tower. Are you sure you are approaching the right runway?" It was in plain view by now, a big white stripe down the middle of it. "Palm Springs tower, Warrior 1-4-7-4 X-ray. The runway is right in front of me. I've done this a few times. I hope by now I know what a runway looks like."

"Warrior 1-4-7-4 X-ray, I think you have the wrong runway. There is a parallel runway on the right, do you have it?" I started looking around. Quite a ways further, there was a runway the size of a postage stamp (in comparison to the runway I was headed for). Off my left wing was a commercial jet that I didn't want to play chicken with.

"Palm Springs tower, Warrior 1-4-7-4 X-ray. Am I supposed to land on that little strip of pavement?" I quickly made the corrections necessary to land on the other runway. No wonder I was too low; I was preparing to land well before I would have had runway.

I got the plane on the ground and made my way to the terminal for private planes. The Palm Springs airport is really great. A couple of guys dressed like golf caddies came out to help me park the plane. It took me a few minutes to regain my composure enough to crawl out on the wing. "Guys, thanks for your help. I just need to sit here for a few minutes."

The pilot that was behind me approaching the runway walked up. "I just had to meet you." I told him this was my first solo cross-country. He could see I was visibly shaken. "This is your solo cross-country!? You did great. You should have seen me the day I took my solo cross-country trip." That made me feel a little better. I was in good company.

After taking a little time to prepare myself, I got back in the plane for the return flight. Taking off is much easier than landing. I was ready for 'easy'. By the time I saw my home airport approaching, I was like a horse going back to the barn. I knew what I needed to do and could execute with confidence. By the time I got back into the terminal, I felt like celebrating. What an accomplishment! And everyone lived to tell about it.

My biggest learning that day happened as I approached the wrong runway. I had to be willing to be wrong and take help from wherever I could get it. How many times do you head down the wrong path and refuse to take sound advice or correct your course, because you're too stubborn to admit you could be wrong? Some situations are a little more life-threatening than others, as I learned that day, but there are no mistakes. Everything happens for a reason. You just need to keep an open mind about any situation.

"Don't put all your eggs in one basket."

How do you know if your mind is open or closed? When you have a problem, do you assume that the outcome will be the same as it was the last time you faced a similar situation? Let's use a really easy example. You're going downtown to a meeting. You are dreading it because you know parking is always a hassle. You always drive around the block several times and finally end up parking in an expensive lot because you can't find an open meter. The open mind knows today can be different.

You visualize what you would like to happen. There is someone pulling away from the curb just as you pull up. You find an inexpensive lot that you haven't noticed before. The universe will make your trip downtown pleasant and successful in every way. Then you celebrate small successes.

In whatever ways things are made easier for you, you acknowledge them. Easy flowing traffic on the freeway, few red lights, a message on a billboard that helps you prepare for the meeting. By the time you get downtown, you will be so full of delight that, even if the parking is still a problem, you'll be able to see the perfection in that too.

Your subconscious is what keeps you on the treadmill, creating the same outcomes. Work your way around that, and things can happen differently. When you open yourself to possibilities, the universe steps in to show you what it's made of. A problem that just moments ago seemed insurmountable suddenly has a virtually unlimited supply of possible solutions. As you start to embrace the vision that this problem could be solved in many ways, your subconscious resistance takes a rest. *"Whew! I don't have to worry so much about this. It seems to be pretty much under control."*

Let's say, for example, your car won't start, and you're wondering how you will get to work. You're trying to generate possibilities for how this problem can be solved. There are so many ways that it doesn't take much to start the process in motion.

Your neighbors could open their garage door the next moment and come to your rescue with jumper cables. The mobile car repair service could happen by after completing a nearby service call. The repairman could have the car running in a matter of moments without even charging you since he was already in the neighborhood. Your spouse could come back to the house to get something needed for his or her offsite meeting, which just happens to be right near your office so you can get a ride. You also could take a moment and see if there's anything *you've* forgotten that might be in the way of your leaving the house. With that out of the way, the car could start on the next turn of the key. Sometimes you need to think really big!

In any challenging situation, there are limitless possibilities of how things could be resolved. The possibilities create pictures in your mind. Since your thoughts create your reality, those pictures go out into the universe and put in motion the law of attraction. Your job is to get busy expecting a favorable outcome and let the universe determine exactly what that looks like. Before you know it, you will have manifested whatever is needed to move you forward on your path.

The goals you create give the universe clear direction. As you begin to execute your action plan, you begin the creation process by chipping away at the subconscious resistance you have to change and to learning a new program. Even with this clear direction and a supportive process, it is important to detach from the desired outcome. There are many alternatives that will be presented to you along the way.

If you choose a path that appears to be taking you somewhere other than where you say you want to go, you make a new choice. You can't really do this if you 'know' exactly how you want things to turn out. When you're attached to a specific outcome, you may miss something that would actually catapult you much more further in your chosen direction.

"It's all in the playing."

Often we are tested by time. We have asked for something to manifest, and it continues to elude us. Do we really trust the process? Do we know that the universe can produce what we want without taking something from others that is rightfully theirs? I have seen so many times how the universe manifests things instantly if everything is in place to accept it.

When something doesn't manifest, something else requires adjustment. It could be something you can control or something you can't. As you explore the situation in more depth, it will become obvious to you that there are things you have or haven't done that keep you from your desires. Are you willing to make the necessary changes to get out of your own way? Sometimes yes, sometimes no. At least, you know you have some control over the situation.

If you haven't made it to New York because you're busy exploring the West Coast, it's easier to accept. At a certain point, you will either actually head east or change your goals. There's no need to dilute your energy on a goal you are obviously not committed to.

When you end up in a very different place from where you thought you were headed, you need to stop and reevaluate. *"How did I get here?"* It won't take long to see how your actions were inconsistent with where you thought you were heading. Sometimes this will just be your subconscious trying to hold you back. The only way to stay on task is to keep going back to your plan.

"What did I say I needed to do to get to where I want to go? What can I do to begin to complete Step One?" With the gift of free will, you have the capacity to make the choices that create your reality. All you need to do is stay aware. Whenever a door closes, a window opens. If you're not on the right path, you'll be given leads to redirect you. The only thing you have to do is commit to looking around until you find it.

Sometimes you'll need to backtrack a little. Have you ever driven down a road a hundred times and just recently noticed something that you never saw before? Maybe you wouldn't have known what meaning it held if you had noticed it the first time past. Now, the 'you that you are at this moment' notices and processes it, using everything you have accumulated up to this point in time. It couldn't have happened one moment sooner. The backtracking was absolutely necessary.

If you get to know yourself, it won't take you long to separate the wheat from the chaff and go forward confidently on your path of choice. You will get there from wherever you are. The only question is how long it will take. How many detours will you have to make before you finally commit to staying focused on the finish line?

I love retracing my steps to see how perfectly orchestrated everything is. The more I look at how I did things, the more I learn and can use the experience in my next challenge. As I go back over the events that ultimately resulted in the perfect outcome, I can see where I made things more or less difficult. I can see the point where I finally got out of the way and let the universe work for me.

"Experience is the mother of all wisdom."

The universe knows nothing but perfection, but that doesn't mean it *feels* perfect when you're in the middle of it. You have to trust the perfection, even when you are really uncomfortable in a situation and discover an open wound, in order to let it go.

Be aware that it's only natural to reach for the 'band-aids'. You know what those are for you. Maybe you spend hours in front of the television or call everyone you know and spend hours on the phone. Some of you might spend all afternoon at the gym.

While any of these activities can be useful at times, you need to watch for how you avoid dealing with what you need to deal with. There is no time like the present to start doing things differently. Instead of taking a defeatist attitude and calling every friend that will listen to you go on about how things aren't working in your life, when you feel that way, pick up a book that is inspirational and remind yourself of the infinite possibilities. Sit in meditation, focusing on staying in the moment. *"There is only now."* Take a walk by yourself and see the beauty that is in everything.

Nature is the perfect canvas for creating your world just the way you want it to be. Whenever I'm feeling a little stuck or off course, there's nothing like a nature walk to put things in perspective. Alone in the vast beauty of nature, all problems shrink to a manageable size. The only company required is Spirit.

A change of scenery can be just what is needed to open up the channels of communication. The body and mind are one. The energy that has been blocking your creative potential is moved out of the way, and possibilities emerge effortlessly. You ask a question, and the answer comes out of the void.

Ask, *"How have I created this situation?"* and you can see your past actions flash across the screen like you're in a movie theater. Ask, *"What do I most need to know now?"* and the next moment produces a very clear message that moves you undeniably forward. Ask, *"Why is this happening?"* and the learning comes quickly so that you can move past the current situation and into whatever the universe has in store for you around the next corner.

Over the last couple of years, I felt led to create a completely new life. Had I known some of the difficulties I would encounter, I would have never put my toe in the water. Sometimes you can't know where you're going or you would be too scared to embark on the journey. Yet, it's been wonderful. I have learned more through the process than I could ever have imagined in the confines of my safe little life.

Every time I encountered seemingly insurmountable odds, I stopped and asked Spirit if I was on the right path. *"Have I missed something? Am I headed in the right direction?"* Very quickly (sometimes within a few moments), the next opportunity presented itself. I simply needed to make some adjustments and had to be brought to a halt in order to see clearly the next turn I needed to make.

It's like traveling on a road that has many hills and valleys. As you reach the top of the hill, you can't see anything beyond the hood of your car. You have to trust that the road continues on the other side. If you stopped every time you were confused or couldn't clearly see where you were going, you'd never get anywhere. The more times you experience what's on the other side of the hill, the easier it becomes to maintain your speed as you approach the top.

Life can be every bit as easy if we just trust the process with fearless faith. As humans, that is difficult. We want to know where we're going and experience things fully every step of the way. We make it hard by choice. We create obstacles to test ourselves and enhance the learning available in the experience. The more we've learned, the quicker we choose the easy path.

"Live and let live."

Discomfort is usually a sign that something really big is trying to work its way into your life. That usually means there are some changes that need to happen in your life to make room for it. At times like these, you can feel the energy building. Rather than resisting, move to faith and trust. It's happening, and you might as well flow with it, making the change gentle and taking some responsibility for how it happens.

Of course, the first few moments spent in a dark room are a little scary. Until your eyes adjust, you can't see anything. Slowly things start to appear as shadows. You see light coming through cracks that weren't there before. Before you know it, you can maneuver almost as well as if there was bright light.

The same holds true with problem-solving. At first, it is really scary, totally dark. There seems to be no way out of the situation. Slowly, you start processing. *"Well, maybe there are ways this situation could be resolved to everyone's satisfaction. If I just adjust a few things, I can see how the solution could manifest easily."* As you practice this, it becomes easier to be patient and trust the process. When you tune in and align with the energy of change, you can channel it, not only for the adjustments that are being made but for whatever else you're trying to accomplish in your life.

For several years before I let go of my old life, I searched for direction. If I was going to give up the known and comfortable, I at least needed to know where I would end up. All I got was, *"Leap and the net will appear,"* over and over, from many different sources (all of whom didn't know me or what I was contemplating). I had to have fearless faith and trust the unknown. The universe would support me if I let go.

It took several years and lots of patience (I'm sure the universe thought many times, "How much confirmation does she need?"), but I finally took that leap and have never regretted it for a moment. My life was limited by the box I had created for myself. I had outgrown it, and there was no choice but to leave it for someone else to grow into. Sort of like a favorite sweater you wore growing up. At a certain point, no matter how perfect it had once seemed, it just didn't fit anymore. Only in hindsight can you fully understand why it had to be the way it was, and the value in that understanding helps you trust more quickly the next time around.

Realizing that you aren't seeing the full picture at any given time is important in dealing with others as well. Have you ever judged others by their actions, saying, "I would never do that?" How can you be sure? Do you know what motivates them and what led to their decision to do whatever they did? You can't possibly know you would *never* do something without having experienced every possible situation.

Other times, when someone does 'wrong' by us, we like to say that the universe will take care of it. "What goes around comes around." Then we wonder why it seems like the person never has to pay for their wrong-doings. It's because *we* are the ones in the wrong. We have no idea what the person came into this lifetime to learn or experience. We can't possibly know how they suffer and what their punishment is.

All we can focus on is ourselves. Are we tolerant and forgiving? Do we give to others what we would like to experience ourselves? I learned a long time ago never to say, "Never." If it slips out now, I am quick to cancel it or accept that I must need to come face to face with something I said I would never do.

You can't worry about how the universe will create things or what faces they will show up with. Your job is to work on yourself. That is a huge job and ultimately will consume so much time that you won't be left with thoughts of judgment or anger.

Chapter 7

Enjoy the Cast of Characters

"All the world's a stage."

To make this journey we call life really fun, you have to find the entertainment value. Walt Disney created the land we all love around life's adventures. But you don't have to go to a theme park to live the adventure. Every activity embraces the universe's awesome creative power. From the simple things to the big demonstration, you have an opportunity to feel like you are part of the process.

I love playing my part in the current theatrical production. I get to decide how big a part I want to play. In the cast of characters, I can be an extra, standing on the sidelines with minimal input. I can play a supporting role, integrally involved but still stepping in and out of the limelight. Or I can play a lead role. I understand that without my being on my toes in every moment, the production will slip and fall. The show will go on, but everyone's experience will be diminished.

At different moments, each of us assumes more or less critical roles. Sometimes, you have to take the lead. At other times, it isn't about you; you are cast in a supporting role.

Whatever role you assume, you need to play your part with conviction. If nothing else, it is preparing you for the next role. You are building the skills you need for the role you came here to play. As you realize this, you begin to understand that you truly have created every experience.

I took a trip to Europe several years ago. It was my first big vacation as the 'new me'. I had always wanted to go to Greece, and this was a perfect opportunity. I wanted to challenge myself with no plans (or expectations), and fortunately, I had a friend that was the perfect companion for this kind of grand adventure. I was a bit delayed in taking the starving college student's version of a trip to Europe, but there was something exciting about the freedom we would have with no reservations. We would decide when we were ready to move on. Of course, I also had the safety net of not actually being a starving college student so, when I needed an infusion of civilization, I was capable of buying it.

We flew to Athens, knowing only that we would fly out of Lisbon several weeks later. We didn't even know where we were headed when we got off the plane. A friend of my travel companion's had told her about one of the Greek islands, Hydra, and we thought we might end up there. After a very long trip with an unscheduled stop in Milan, we were dumped out at the dock where the boats which took travelers between islands departed. At this point, Hydra seemed like as good a Greek island as any.

Hydra turned out to be just what I needed. There was nothing industrialized about it, not even motorized vehicles. In fact, they sent a donkey for our luggage. We went to the tourist office and were directed to a small hotel that was well-hidden from any foot traffic. We checked in and immediately felt like a welcome addition to the family. The hotel owner seemed to delight in helping us fully experience the island. It was absolutely incredible.

We wanted to be able to take it home with us. Instead, we took plenty of photos. Most of the trip's story is told with a view of the backs of our heads. When we asked someone to take our picture, they usually had to stand behind us so the picture would capture the moment's scene.

After a few days exploring Hydra, we began to think about moving on. We asked the hotel's owner for recommendations on how best to experience the mainland of Greece. He planned the perfect trip for us. We would tour the Peloponnese peninsula with its ancient castle and experience Greece as few tourists do. Everything seemed perfect. The boat from Hydra would take us to exactly where we needed to go. The transfer would be easy.

The only problem was me. I couldn't let go of 'my plan'. I was attached to what I thought a trip to Greece should include. I thought I had to see Athens and the Acropolis. Rather than seeing what I was supposed to see, I insisted on seeing what I thought I needed to see. We headed to Athens and were shocked back to reality. It was too much of a culture shock after several days on Hydra. We spent one day touring the city and couldn't wait to leave.

I was reminded that things can turn out more difficult than they need to if you ignore the leads given to you by the universe. In Athens, even something as simple as manifesting some Spanikopita turned difficult. It seemed to be always just beyond our reach. When we got back to the U.S., it was everywhere. (We did discover the giant white beans, however... giant white beans shaped liked limas and about as large as a nice-sized oyster. We're still talking about them.)

Anyway, we were like caged animals. We would do whatever we had to do to get out of the city.

We knew our next stop was Italy. Since we were taking the overnight boat, we began the journey. There were several modes of public transportation between where we were and our next destination. By the time we landed in Brindisi, Italy, it had been a couple of days since we had had a shower and a decent meal. Our plan was to take the overnight train from Brindisi to Napoli, so there wasn't much we could do about a shower. We had to settle for a good meal.

It was the middle of the afternoon, and our choices were limited. We found a neighborhood café and, since there wasn't much business at that time of day, the owner sat down with us to chat. We started sharing our experiences and plans. He had a great idea – a drinking game.

I hadn't played a drinking game since college. The game was 'Truth and Drink'. I was first. When confronted with a question I wasn't inclined to answer, I said, "I'll just drink." (We had a nice bottle of Chianti that had accompanied our lunch, and it wasn't too threatening to enjoy a little more.)

He was quick to clarify things. This was his game, and the rules were a little different from what I had experienced in college. 'Truth and Drink'. You answer the question truthfully, and then you drink. An afternoon of his game, and you were intimate friends.

We were feeling pretty satisfied a couple of hours later, when he started telling us about the party they had planned on the beach that evening. It was someone's birthday, and he assured us that we wouldn't want to miss it. He even offered to help us find a room so that our stay would be comfortable.

He said we didn't really want to take the overnight train. There were professional thieves that would spray something in your cabin to make you sleep. Once you were out, they would rob you blind.

Surely this man just wanted us to stay for the party so he was making it sound worse than it really was. Besides, that couldn't happen to *us*. We were divinely protected. Even though he had been very nice and seemed genuinely concerned about us, the truth is that I was attached (again) to our plan, so we made our way to the train station.

The train pulled in, and we found a decent cabin that a nice, young Italian man was already sitting in. We were new to this Eurail stuff so we didn't understand that we would have to share the cabin with other people. Still, he certainly wasn't threatening, so we made ourselves comfortable. The train began its journey to Napoli.

What seemed like a short while later, I woke up to see that the young man that was originally sitting in our cabin was gone and another was rifling through our luggage. He had taken our bags down from the upper rack and was making quick work of them.

I startled my friend awake with, "He's got your purse!" She jumped up, and he pushed her back down. In the most amazing burst of bravery I've ever experienced, I jumped up and slammed him against the wall of the train. I felt like I was living a cartoon, in the role of Penelope Pitstop. I started screaming, "Help, help, help us!"

A big brawny man came to our rescue. We chased the thief up and down the cars and finally pinned him against the wall by his neck. He had our things stuffed everywhere. As the train pulled into the next station, he squirmed free and escaped.

By this time, the conductor had arrived on the scene and tried to help us as much as he could, given the language barrier. We searched the adjacent cabins and found our belongings spread along what must have been their familiar route. We recovered everything, with the exception of my friend's wallet. Thank God for traveler's checks.

At the next stop, a new passenger tried to join us in our cabin, and we looked at the conductor with sheer terror in our eyes. He sent the person on his way, apparently telling him to find another place to sit, and kept a close watch over us for the remainder of the trip. We sat wide-eyed for the rest of the night, anxiously awaiting Napoli.

After the night we had just experienced, it is no wonder my friend was less than excited by the prospect of getting on the bus that would take us to Amalfi. I knew we didn't want to spend another night in undesirable surroundings, and that meant we needed to move through Napoli quickly. So, we were off.

I was beginning to see the error of my ways. We had missed what I knew was a great opportunity to see mainland Greece through the eyes of a local because I was attached to seeing Athens. I obviously still hadn't learned my lesson when I insisted that we skip the beach party (and a nice comfortable place to spend the night) and move on to Napoli by overnight train. In hindsight, we were protected; we'd been offered the signs. We just chose to ignore them.

When we got to Amalfi, I was ecstatic to turn the trip over to Spirit and trust that we would be sent whoever was assigned to assist us in the moment. It never fails; you are sent exactly what (and who) you need in order to experience the next moment.

"There is a time and a place for everything."

If you are paying attention, you will be shown definitively which direction to turn. What I find the most delightful is to go looking for something, only to be led to something else. I might be looking for something that is easily attainable today, but the universe knows that tomorrow – or in the near future – I am going to be in search of something else. When I'm watching and listening along the way, my journey is effortless.

"Where to next, Spirit?" Before you ask, you have been answered. Tomorrow's 'to-

do list' is taken care of today, often in a display of the universe's awesome powers of synchronicity.

Not too long ago, I traveled to the state of Washington for a trade show. When I left home, I was pretty upset. I had just had an encounter with someone who knew exactly how to push my buttons and seemed to take every opportunity to do just that.

I knew I should be able to shake off this feeling, but nothing I tried was working. The trade show started the next day, and I had to be ready to spend the day chatting with people and being personable. That was the farthest thing from my current reality. *"Spirit, I need an attitude adjustment. This is bigger than me. I need your help."*

I read in a magazine that there was a vegetarian wine bar nearby, and I hoped an early dinner and a good night's sleep would take care of things. I drove around for what seemed like an hour and couldn't find the place I was looking for. I finally saw a place that looked like it was a decent substitute and parked the car.

As I got out of the car, a young man approached me to apologize for cutting me off. I told him that wasn't necessary since I was so lost I hadn't even noticed, but he was insistent.

As I walked into the place I was headed, I realized that it wasn't at all what I was looking for. It *did* serve a purpose though. I asked the bartender if he knew of the vegetarian wine bar I was looking for. He told me it was great and right down the street. I had passed it several times.

By now, the apologetic young man and his friend were sitting next to me and overheard my conversation with the bartender. He said, "That's not really where you want to go." He told me that he knew where I would be most comfortable and then gave me directions.

When I thanked him and said I'd try the vegetarian place first, he invited himself along. We would check out the vegetarian wine bar and then walk over to the place he recommended. I had asked for an attitude adjustment. Was this it?

After a quick stop at the first place, we headed to the restaurant he had recommended. And, of course, he was right! It was perfect, exactly what I needed.

By the end of the evening, my attitude was adjusted well beyond what I had hoped for. I got back to my room and woke up the next morning ready to greet the day and anyone that wanted to join me in it. It can be so easy when you're open to whatever and whomever the universe sends to assist with your request.

"There's no time like the present."

We've talked a lot about getting exactly what you need. The sooner you accept that you need the current experience (even if it's uncomfortable) and that it has come to serve you in some way, the better off you'll be. In these moments, I ask what I need to learn and embrace the opportunity to move through it, quickly if possible. Sometimes what we want is actually what we need.

Let's say you've been asking the universe to manifest a new job for you. Things start to move; you start to see signs that the new opportunity is coming. In a totally unexpected way, you are offered a position that appears to be perfectly suited for you. You let go of the old job and move forward knowing that this is exactly what you've asked for.

Two days on the new job, and you're questioning everything. It isn't at all what you thought it would be. You got what you wanted; now you have to want what you got. Maybe you need to let go of your expectations.

When you created the new job in your mind, it looked a certain way. Is the reality different and feeling a bit uncomfortable? Be careful what you ask for; you are sure to get it. You made your bed, and now you have to lay in it. But keep in mind there is always something to be learned and there is always help available to you.

When you reach a point in your life where you know something just isn't working, it creates a heavy, dark influence. Some situations are a continual drain, even after you have tweaked things and made whatever adjustments seemed appropriate. At this point, it's easy to feel defeated and fall prey to negativity. All you know is that you have a problem and need to move in the direction of solving it.

That means it's time to shake things up. If you don't move in a new direction yourself, the universe will take care of things for you. But it's easier if *you* begin the process. While letting go might be scary, there *is* light on the other side.

If no move feels like the right move and you aren't sure which way to turn, ask for help. As long as you are holding on to what isn't working, it is taking up space in your life. You have to clear the way for something new. Ask yourself why you're holding on. What could you do to begin the process of releasing what isn't working?

Send the universe a message that you're serious. You know things need to shift, and you're willing to play your part. No genuine need goes unfilled. When you let go of something that isn't working for you, a vacuum is created. The universe will send you clear direction and whatever you need to make the shift. Your challenge is to take a deep breath and trust the empty space. You need to be able to step back and see the big picture.

"Take a look at the big picture."

Have you ever been watching a movie and saw a character preparing to make what is obviously a really bad choice? As a member of the audience, it's much easier to see the big picture and what it will take to move in the 'right' direction. You think, "No – don't do it! Just turn around, say 'No!'. Kiss the girl," or whatever the case may be. So you basically just need to become the audience of your own life. But how?

The techniques we've talked about in this book will help you do that. When you feel the anxiety building to make a decision, your gut will tell you that there is something you're missing. The more you allow yourself to buy in to worry and fear, the farther away you will drift from shore. Instead, take a walk, meditate, write; do anything but what seems like a quick fix to eliminate the anxiety.

A few hours in nature always lightens my mood. I feel connected. I am reminded that I am an integral part of something magnificent. How can I be concerned with anything but here and now when confronted head on with the universe's perfection?

You know yourself well enough by now to know if what you choose to do will actually make you feel good or if it is simply a band-aid or addictive behavior. Do something that makes you feel good. The process moves you off the stage and into the audience. You'll gain access to facts that had been eluding you. When you do make a decision, it won't come from anxiety. It will be born of confidence and faith.

Every choice you make helps to create the current version of who you are. If you can seize the moment and move forward, then your creative energy can be put to use elsewhere. Everything you say you want to do sucks energy. Some things use a little, some a lot. Rather than spending energy creating a new opportunity to manifest what you say you want, move on to other things. The opportunity will reappear. It may be disguised with a different face and new characters, but it is the same story.

"What goes around comes around."

We can see this with movie story lines. Sometimes the recurring plot is cleverly disguised, and you have to really think about it to recognize the similarities. Other times they go ahead and call it a remake so you don't have to wonder. Either way it is the same story – your opportunity knocking.

You know when you've been down a road before. There are the same signs. When you recognize it, you have the option to make the same choice with similar consequences or to create a different outcome by changing your character's lines. In the past, you kept going straight when you clearly needed to take a left. You might have been able to get away with avoiding this turn the last couple of times, but you know now that one more time past the turn and you'll miss an opportunity that has been cleverly orchestrated just for you.

These are the times in your life when you know, *"This is it! If I don't make the decision that is consistent with my plans and goals, it will reverberate through my whole life."* Every cell of your being is supercharged with energy. Seize the moment – it defines you. Use this boost of energy to help you move through the resistance and the blocks that keep you trapped in your familiar box.

When everything fell away that was keeping me from moving to Colorado, I knew that I was confronting a major turning point in my life. Everything I said I wanted was being offered to me, and I had to let go of the known and familiar to pull it into my life. I knew if I didn't make the decision to move, things would get complicated again and my window of opportunity would close. There was no telling how long it would be before it opened again.

I had asked for this. Now I just prayed that it would be everything I imagined it would be. The universe supported me every step of the way. It wasn't gentle, but I was provided with everything I needed to create a new life. If I had chosen to delay the move further, it would still have remained as part of my life's desires.

In creating your action plan, you gave yourself very clear directions for getting to where you say you want to go. Your choices either support that or indicate that you're headed in a different direction. If you do not take the opportunity that is put before you, will it forever alter the course of your life? You can't know for sure, but I believe that you will end up exactly where you are supposed to be. The big question is how difficult the journey will be.

"Ask and ye shall receive."

When you get exactly what you've been asking for, it's time to act. The universe has answered your call and even provided a guide for you… a messenger to help you move through your resistance and support you as you take off in a new direction. Perhaps it comes to you in the words of a song on the radio, an idle chat with a store clerk, someone taking your hand and leading you through it, or even a dream.

I have had the opportunity to work with dreams quite a bit as I've moved through this life adventure. Dreams are an amazing thing. They are symbolic of what your subconscious is focused on. If you try to interpret a dream literally, there is a good chance that you will end up way out in left field. By looking at each character as an aspect of yourself, you can peel it apart and begin to understand what your subconscious is trying to tell you.

Some people say they don't dream. It isn't that they don't dream. Just like anything else you want to develop, it takes a bit of focused effort. You spend a little time before going to sleep, asking for your subconscious to give you a message. You prepare yourself by putting a notebook or tape recorder by the bed. You won't have much time if you want to capture the rich details. As you awake, you need to recognize that you have been in the middle of a vivid dream and take care not to move too much until you feel you have begun to capture it. Stay in it and begin going over the details. When you feel like you're ready, start writing or recording.

There are great books that help you interpret your dreams. The most important thing to remember is that they are *your* dreams. If someone else interprets your dream and it doesn't feel right for you, then it isn't right. Ask yourself, *"If I knew what the dream was trying to tell me, what would it be?"* Your subconscious will then go to work to answer the question.

I use a technique that was shared with me by a psychologist I worked with. For anyone that has nightmarish dreams, this method can sound pretty scary, but it has never failed me. The scene can become even comical. And it really is exhilarating to take your power back.

Let's say, for example, that you are having a recurrent dream where you're being chased. You can go back into that dream in meditation and stop running. You turn around and face what you fear. At that point, you can ask the characters in the dream why they are chasing you. When you turn around and confront what is chasing you, the energy goes away. After using this technique myself a couple of times, there was no energy in the chase. Now, my subconscious just doesn't go there. The dream comes in a much more friendly way.

It's just another example of what an incredible tool meditation is. When you meditate, you experience a place and time where you can truly know you're not alone, a welcome relief from all the time we spend alone in a crowd in this world.

Throughout the years, I have gone through phases in my meditation that have provided me with exactly what I needed at the time. I have experienced meditation that has been much more real than anything I can touch and feel. What I have discovered over time is that each of my guides (from my original 'guide', through what I call the power circle, to my current relationship with a faceless energy source) has come to serve a purpose. When that purpose has been served, they move on and are replaced by one who will provide me with the guidance I need at the moment.

Not long ago, I was entering my meditation and was clearly directed away from where I normally 'go'. My comfortable place is an altar in the middle of a room with two doors on each wall. Each door provides a different scene to work with and I never know what (or who) is going to turn up.

This day, I was guided to another place. It felt comfortable and somewhat familiar, but I still missed the known scenario of my altar and special doors. I asked why I couldn't go back there. I was told I didn't need the 'props'. I had become dependent on the scene and needed to experience the freedom of not knowing where I was going.

I practiced without my familiar scene for several months. One day, I realized that I had done what I needed to do. I wasn't dependent on the scene. Now I could go back there if I wanted and not lose anything in the process.

I can't stress enough that the universe will guide you wherever you need to go, to learn what you need to learn and experience what you need to experience. When you use the tools available to you, pay attention to the signs, enjoy the cast of characters, and revel in how the scene unravels, your path will be full of delight.

Chapter 8
Gratitude

"Where there is wonder and adventure, there is growth."

Life is an adventure, sometimes a more enjoyable adventure than at other times. When the adventure is challenging and the road is a little bumpier, you may have to stretch to delight in the moment. This presents you with an opportunity to demonstrate gratitude.

Moving directly to gratitude is the quickest way to alter a challenging experience. All it takes is trusting that you are exactly where you are supposed to be in every moment. *"Spirit, I am grateful for every experience."* If you have done your homework and can accept that there is a plan, no matter how convoluted it may feel at the time, then it is easy to be grateful.

Once you move to gratitude, everything begins to fall into place. It is almost like the universe (or actually your higher self) is testing you. How far have you come on your journey? What have you learned? Where do you still need work? I find that I am much quicker to leap to that place now than I was five years ago, but I still have lots of road to travel.

"Two wrongs don't make a right."

I still find myself wallowing at times. Most often this happens when I encounter a stupid rule or procedure. The way I look at it, these rules are made to be broken. If there is a rule that doesn't have room for adjustment, then it is sure to be quickly challenged by a situation that leads to it being blown out of the water.

One of the stupid rules I really have a problem with has to do with checking your bags at the airport. If the airlines really want to motivate people to check their luggage, then they need to prioritize baggage handling. They pride themselves on arriving on time, but you still end up waiting around while they move your luggage.

Sure, at some airports your bags are waiting for you on the carousel by the time you have walked there from departing the plane. But in the Las Vegas airport, for example, you consistently wait 30 minutes or more for the bags to arrive to be claimed. By no coincidence, it was at an airline ticket counter that I got to see for the first time, from the perspective of a bystander, how 'Mr. Nasty' affects everyone involved.

Last year, I took a friend to the airport and accompanied him to the ticket counter. He had missed an earlier flight and was attempting to make it back to Las Vegas for one of his daughter's functions at school. Being 'Donuts with Dads', it wasn't like he wouldn't be missed if he didn't make it.

The ticket agent told him he would have to check his carry-on bag. Of course, the ticket agent didn't know the situation and had no idea how critical that was. If my friend checked his bag, he would surely not make it to the school in time to be with his daughter. Even though the carry-on bag was indisputably a carry-on, the clerk had obviously been instructed to attempt to have as many bags checked as possible.

My friend started out explaining nicely that it was critical that he be allowed to carry his bag on the flight. The agent dug in his heels and insisted that my friend check his bag. Finally, my friend slammed his bag down on the counter and walked away.

We were all so startled that it took us a minute to regain our composure. I was still standing there, so I felt obliged to try to smooth things over. I told the agent that my friend was trying to make it home to meet a commitment with his daughter and, if he checked the bag, he wouldn't make it. As it was, everything had to fall into place perfectly to have a chance.

The agent, still a little shocked from my friend's reaction, agreed to allow him to carry on the bag. When my friend calmed down and returned to continue the discussion, I told him that the agent had agreed to let him carry on the bag. The agent told my friend that his behavior was unnecessary and wasn't the reason he changed his mind.

This didn't seem like the time to make a point, but I wholeheartedly disagreed. I watched as the entire situation unfolded, and there is no question in my mind. Nothing less than this shocking and unexpected reaction from my friend would have changed the tide.

More importantly, though, I learned something very valuable in the exchange. I saw how each party played a role in the scene. I could stand in everyone's shoes and see how their actions were entirely appropriate from their point of view, how their actions affected everyone around them, and how they were personally affected.

Both sides wanted things their own way and were willing to fight for what they believed in. It is a human reaction to defend yourself, yet it could have consumed so much less energy had it been handled differently. I knew I would not be able to participate in an encounter like this in the future without feeling it from all the angles.

This experience also reminded me how a person with a difficult attitude can put a damper on your day. At the same time, an encounter with a bright, cheerful person can alter your day for the better, so the goal is to try to do that for others. You do have a choice. It isn't just fight or flight. You can choose light. Every time you choose love and light, it spreads a little further.

Like attracts like. When you want to attract positive, charming people into your life, you need to be positive and charming yourself. Even though I know this, it's one of the most difficult things for me to practice. I do really well until I happen on a clerk that is mindlessly attempting to enforce one of these 'stupid rules'.

I was at a café in the grocery store the other day. The place is laid out poorly and just doesn't flow. You end up having to stand in line with several clerks to make all your purchases. It doesn't make sense to me that the customer should be inconvenienced because the store is unorganized.

I asked the clerk to print something for me, so I could combine my purchases, and it turned into even more of a hassle than the already disorganized mess I was in the middle of. When something doesn't work quite as easily as I think it should, I get aggravated and frustrated. Impatience gets the better of me, and it shows. As a result of my reaction, the clerk had to deal with her own experience of the encounter.

"Practice makes perfect."

In the moments after a time like this, you reflect on what you did and how you strayed so far off course. *"Why would I let something so trivial get to me? I deal with far more life-threatening situations than this with much more grace."* It's then that you realize you have more work to do. It's just one step at a time.

Once you know what you need to work on, you can be confident you will do better the next time. *"I will recognize the feeling that shows up in my body and smile through it. When my buttons are pushed, I will choose my battle."* In every situation, you can ask, *"Is this important enough to take a stand?"*

These experiences challenge you to turn over control of the situation. If you try to micromanage things, you will end up in certain mediocrity. When you let it go, you are wonderfully rewarded. A great example comes from the ongoing saga of my European vacation.

We arrived in Amalfi on a Saturday in late June. This is significant because it's the equivalent of trying to go to San Diego for the Fourth of July with no reservations. We checked several hotels and were turned away; there was 'no room at the inn'. At the last one, I told the desk clerk that we were just going to sit in the lobby until they came up with someplace for us to stay.

It didn't take them long. We were summarily dismissed to a small inn where the room was no bigger than the two twin beds that lined the walls. It did have a private bath, and by this time, my whole day was made with the appearance of a blow dryer that worked on European current. I knew we had to find a more habitable place to stay, but right then, I had more important things to think about.

It had been several days since we had had a good night's sleep. We were beginning to feel a bit shell-shocked, as we fully acknowledged the after-effects of the overnight train trip to Napoli. It was late afternoon, and a nice meal sounded like a step in the right direction. We would think about getting a good night's sleep later. I wasn't so sure we could get a good night's sleep at the closet we were calling home, but at least we were clean.

We left the inn in search of the perfect restaurant. We found an incredible place that overlooked Amalfi Bay. It took us a while to shift back to civilization, but we soon started chatting with a couple that was sitting at the table next to us.

It turned out that they were also from America and were staying at a hotel just outside of town. The hostess at the restaurant happened to be the hotel owner's daughter, and our new friends asked her to call and request a room for us. There was one room available, and we said we'd take it. We went back to the closet, packed our bags, and were checked into the most amazing place I've ever been a couple of hours later.

I'm not sure if it was as incredible as I remember it or if we had just lowered our expectations to the point where anything would have seemed like the lap of luxury. OK, on second thought, it *was* incredible. Every morning, we would greet the day overlooking the ocean from the terrace cafe. After breakfast, we would take the elevator down the cliff to the pool. The attendants made sure we had everything we needed to make our day relaxing and comfortable.

Upon first seeing the room, I was so grateful. It had a real bathroom, with a shower that wasn't a shared home for the toilet. It had been a bit difficult for me to comprehend the widely-accepted European practice of putting the toilet in the shower. I guess it is an efficient use of space, but you are challenged to make sure you find a dry place for the toilet paper.

We slept for 14 hours the first night. When we woke up the next day, we walked into town to do a little exploring. We ended up at a restaurant for a late afternoon snack, and the waiter invited us back for dinner that evening. Still travel-lagged and recovering from the train debacle, we had to motivate ourselves to go anywhere. By the time we finished dinner, we were perfectly satisfied with the idea of going back to our little haven and sleeping our way to another glorious day.

Life changes in a moment. As we finished our glasses of wine, a group of people walked into the restaurant. We could sense this was no ordinary group of people. It wasn't about appearances but just a feeling. The next thing we knew, we had been invited over to their table and were part of the family. We all left together and headed to their favorite after-dinner spot.

Our new friends led the way to a Karaoke bar under the church in the plaza in Amalfi. By day, this church was quite a showpiece. The entire face was covered with gold tile, in a mosaic display that took your breath away. When the afternoon sun caught it, you were transported to another world.

At the bar, one of the men performed an Italian version of Frank Sinatra that left you begging for more. We closed the place at around two in the morning. The only thing that motivated us to get up later that morning was the closing time of the breakfast buffet. The perfection repeated itself every night. I felt like we were being rewarded for having dealt with the train thief and not letting it ruin our vacation. What a life! Why leave? Does it get any better than this?

I will never forget Amalfi. After several days there, I had asked one of our new friends why I felt so content and relaxed. She said there was something in the air. As long as you remained in Amalfi, you would be in somewhat of a trance. Once you left, you would quickly feel discontented and back to 'normal'. If the rest of the world was 'normal', I wanted no part of it.

Eventually, though, the friend I was traveling with asked me if we were ever going to leave. It hadn't occurred to me. I guess we did have to move on at some point. I told her I needed a couple of days to prepare myself. Like I said before, life is an adventure. When the adventure includes beautiful scenery and total relaxation, it is easy to experience the pleasure in the situation.

"Experience is the best teacher."

Upon reflection, I realized how much I had learned by this point in our journey. When I left the island of Hydra in Greece, I was so attached to my plan to visit Athens that I had missed what I know would have been a life-altering experience. We thought we knew *how* Spirit was protecting us when we insisted on getting on the overnight train to Napoli, only to find that our protection was right there in the restaurant we visited. We were given every reason to stay and insisted on sticking to 'our' plan.

I had been shown that the most valuable and pleasant experiences were the ones that I hadn't planned. I was grateful for the little things. Something as simple as a blow dryer could put a smile on my face for a whole afternoon.

I had needed the full range of experiences to realize this and learn what I needed to learn. Back then it had to be dramatic. Thank God I learn a bit more gently now. I don't need quite the same jolt.

We left Amalfi and headed for Firenze. We remained in an altered state (although no longer in the Amalfi trance). We knew that wherever we went and whatever we experienced was uniquely perfect. We were grateful for every experience. It was a new beginning. I began to live life differently, always checking back to see if I am attached to my own agenda or allowing Spirit to create the current version of magnificent.

That's not to say there won't be obstacles, but by now you know that obstacles serve a useful purpose in moving you forward on the right course. If you stray a bit too far right, you encounter an obstacle that pushes you back to the left. Maybe you have been moving too quickly and are missing some of the juice along the way. Obstacles can provide you with just what you need to slow down enough to smell the roses.

As I worked through learning to trust universal intelligence in every moment, I found that it was difficult for me to allow myself time to process. How could I 'walk my talk' and still give myself the space to wallow a bit in the moment? I began to realize that, if I didn't take time to honor my emotions, I missed a great opportunity. There is nothing like a period of wallowing in self-pity to make you know that's not where you want to live. And there is a lot of learning available in that space of creative tension.

We have all seen people that have to 'hit bottom' before they begin to turn their lives around. When they do, great things happen. They are in many ways reborn. You can use this same energy without even getting close to hitting bottom.

By allowing yourself a limited period of wallowing, you get the best of all worlds. You realize all the learning that is available to you in the situation that made you feel like wallowing in the first place. Sometimes, it just gives you the space to see the other ways that Spirit has brought joy into your life.

Whenever you are confronted with a situation that you are having difficulty finding the perfection in, say to yourself, *"I know (and trust) that this moment is perfect. I can hardly wait to see what comes from this situation!"* You are immediately catapulted into a positive state of expectancy. You are reminded of prior questionable experiences where things worked out perfectly, better than you ever could have imagined.

As soon as you acknowledge the perfection, the universe steps in to show you *how* it is uniquely perfect. When you are shown how this is perfect, it is yet more confirmation and support for future moments of challenged perfection.

When you bless this moment, the universe will return nothing but blessings. Personally, I get constant pleasure from the universe, and I delight in watching it work. It bears reminding: Nothing is all good, nothing is all bad.

"Things aren't always what they seem."

When you are challenged to find your way to gratitude, an inspiring story can be just the thing to bring you back to a place of gratitude and trust. This story, circulated far and wide via the Internet, is a perfect example.

> *Two traveling angels stopped to spend the night in the home of a wealthy family. The family was rude and refused to let the angels stay in the mansion's guest room. Instead, the angels were given a small space in the cold basement.*
>
> *As they made their bed on the hard floor, the older angel saw a hole in the wall and repaired it. When the younger angel asked why, the older angel replied, "Things aren't always what they seem."*
>
> *The next night, the pair came to rest at the house of a very poor, but very hospitable, farmer and his wife. After sharing what little food they had, the couple let the angels sleep in their bed where they could have a good night's rest.*
>
> *When the sun came up the next morning, the angels found the farmer and his wife in tears. Their only cow, whose milk had been their sole source of income, lay dead in the field.*
>
> *The younger angel was infuriated and asked the older angel, "How could you have let this happen? The first man had everything, yet you helped him," she accused. "The second family had little but was willing to share everything, and you let the cow die."*
>
> *"Things aren't always what they seem," the older angel replied. "When we stayed in the basement of the mansion, I noticed there was gold stored in that hole in the wall. Since the owner was so obsessed with greed and unwilling to share his good fortune, I sealed the wall so he wouldn't find it.*
>
> *Then last night as we slept in the farmer's bed, the angel of death came for his wife. I gave him the cow instead. Things aren't always what they seem."*

Keep this in mind when things don't turn out the way you want or the way you think they should. You need to trust that every outcome is always in your best interest. You just might not see *how* until some later time. When you can keep this perspective, it is much easier to practice gratitude, even in the face of challenges in your life.

Your goal is to be grateful in every moment of every day, to be able to reach a state of gratitude on auto-pilot. As you begin to weave gratitude into all your actions and interactions, it gets easier if you find a sort of entertaining ritual that helps you give thanks regularly. I say, *"Thank you, Spirit,"* when I am approaching a traffic light and it remains green long enough to allow me to continue on my journey unhindered. I do the same for parking spots, beautiful days, and great meals. The more I am grateful for, the more I have to be grateful for. It's fun to watch obstacles move out of my way, and it begins to feel like the universe is having a great time helping me out.

The more time I spend in this space, the easier it is to see opportunities to be grateful in more challenging situations. A parking spot doesn't appear where I thought it would and I say, *"Spirit, I know there is a reason that I am not finding a spot right now. Show me where I need to be."* More than likely, the lack of a parking spot has been provided to adjust my course. If I'm paying attention, I make the adjustment that I need to make and get back to a slightly altered version of my original plan.

Every opportunity that you take to jump to gratitude chips away at the old subconscious programming that keeps you dipping into the same disappointing well. Each time you practice gratitude for the small things that manifest in your life, you are actually training your subconscious to expect only things you are grateful for to manifest – ultimately creating what you expect. It's a self-fulfilling prophecy of monumental importance.

As part of this reprogramming, I begin my affirmations and goals by giving thanks as if they have already manifested or been realized. *"I give thanks that I attract like-minded companions everywhere I go."*

So, in phrasing your affirmations, first give thanks to the universe. Then also acknowledge that, before you have even asked, your request has been granted. It has already happened, and no one lost anything in the process. No one else has to have anything less than all their desires fulfilled in order for your desires to manifest. The universe is perfectly capable of creating win/win, as long as you remind yourself in the process that you desire only what is in the best interest and for the highest good of all concerned.

I have found that manifesting is much easier (and quicker) when the universe has fewer people to juggle. Can you imagine what it takes to facilitate a chance encounter? Just getting me to the right place at the right time requires precision (and I really try to pay attention). Add to that everything that needs to be orchestrated with the other party or parties, and you can see how complicated things can be. Think of all the little things that could get in the way. Even if those little obstacles actually alter today's plan perfectly, they potentially require the universe to restart the process of putting together the chance encounter from scratch.

If I am working on manifesting something that requires little more than a simple juggling act (as opposed to the three-ring circus that is usually underway), my desire appears before my eyes, sometimes so quickly that it scares me a little. Such was the case in the story I related earlier about not having time to get to the post office when I needed something mailed. Almost before I asked, a mail truck appeared to take the package off my hands. *"Wow!! The universe really hears me."* I understood in that moment the importance of being careful what you ask for.

"Judge not, lest ye be judged."

Whatever you focus on energetically will grow. This is a universal law, and it doesn't matter whether it is something you would admit to wanting to attract into your life or not. A situation can only be 'bad' if you say it's 'bad'. Since nothing is all good or all bad, then you can find good in every situation. Find the good, and it will miraculously turn around.

If you condemn something or dwell on an encounter that you would have liked to see played out differently, you put energy into it. Instead, let it go. Trust that, if you need to do it again, it will be presented to you another time. Spend a few moments imagining what you would do differently, seeing a more positive outcome, and knowing that, somewhere in the universe, you have been acknowledged.

It's all in the way you look at things. My favorite word of late is 'interesting'. Rather than judging something as good or bad, it is interesting. It's a fairly safe word if used with pure intention.

When you live life like I do, with a zealous curiosity, you notice everything. You want to know the motivation behind someone's actions or reactions. If you observe a person in reaction to their own circumstances and react with judgment rather than detached curiosity, you will inevitably be faced with a similar situation. You'll find yourself challenged to make a choice that you could have never imagined yourself making.

The alternative is to find the actions of others interesting, without judging them. You can imagine that there are many facts that contribute to their decision-making process that you are unaware of. Given all the facts and the unique circumstances, there is a good chance that you might act in a similar fashion or, maybe even by your own standards, worse.

In any kind of relationship, you are playing with fire if you expect someone to change. Actually expecting change isn't the risky part, because you know people will change. Where you get into trouble is when you expect that they will change in the way that you would like to see them change. People change as they grow, but growth is a very personal thing.

You have no idea what journey another person's soul is on, and you have enough to deal with trying to manage your own. If you expect that someone is going to finally 'get it' and the result will be the person you have always known they could be, you are sure to be enlightened otherwise. At some point, they will 'get it' (even if not in this lifetime).

In the meantime, consider the person that they are (and also are becoming) simply interesting. That will give you the opportunity to accept them just the way they are and be grateful for whatever they contribute to your life. And the more gratitude you express for every experience, the more you will find to be grateful for.

Chapter 9
Don't Force It

"Old habits die hard."

The word 'paradigm' is probably familiar to you. It was first brought to public attention during the 1960's by the scientist and historian, Thomas S. Kuhn, in his influential and controversial book, The Structure of Scientific Revolutions. Kuhn observed that a group of universally-recognized scientific principles provide a model (or paradigm) for problem-solving for a time but are eventually displaced by a new perception of how the world works.

As scientists conduct experiments, they regularly encounter surprise results that don't fit with the assumptions of the current model. They either have to find ways to explain these unexpected results in terms of the prevailing paradigm or, when that fails to work, construct a new paradigm.

When you decide to pursue the path to a new life, one open to the wisdom and guidance of the universe, these same principles apply. You experiment with something new and, oftentimes, the results surprise you. At that point, you have to take another look at the paradigm you have been working with over the course of your life and determine if the results fit or if, in fact, you need to develop a new paradigm for the 'new you'. When new results don't fit with old ways of thinking, you can't force it. It's time to make some changes.

I've already shared with you some details of how my European vacation created a paradigm shift for me, but there's more to the story. In the last chapter, we had left Amalfi on our way to Firenze.

We arrived in Firenze after a pleasant train ride, a welcome contrast to our last experience on a train. We wanted to do a bit of sightseeing in the city and then tour the wine country the next day. The hotel concierge arranged for a driver to escort us through the wine country. We were expecting a day of beautiful scenery, vineyard tours, and wine tasting.

Several hours into the journey, we realized that our expectations might have been a bit unrealistic. While the countryside was incredibly beautiful, touring the Italian wine country is nothing like touring California's Napa region. The vineyards don't invite passers-by in for tasting. There was a bit of a language barrier with the driver, and we found the alternatives limited. We did finally stop for lunch in a quaint tourist town, but the whole experience was not at all what we had expected or planned.

Yet there was so much to see and experience, if we could let go of what we thought we would see and do. It was yet another great learning experience on the journey, just one more thing to let go of. With no expectations, there can be no disappointments.

We knew we wanted to make our way to Portugal next, but we had no idea where we would end up in the meantime. Dark was approaching when we got off the train in Genoa. Since there was no way we were going to try our luck with the overnight train again, we found a suitable place to stay and explored the area a bit. To get to Portugal, we had to go through France so, the next day, we caught the train that would take us there.

The south of France was stunning, and we decided to stop for a couple of days and see what it had to offer us. I think I must have had an unpleasant past-life experience in France, because I have never been comfortable there. This time was no different. I couldn't wait to leave. In fact, we decided that we wanted out quickly and that we'd had about enough of train travel. I called and booked us a flight to Lisbon.

The next day we were at the Algarve coast. It was beautiful, but we were finally missing the comforts of home. We decided to see if we could change our flight back to the States so we could arrive in New York a couple of days earlier than originally planned. *"Thank you, Spirit."* We found a helpful agent and were scheduled to leave the next day.

One last night in Portugal… As we walked around that afternoon, we discovered a wonderful little port-cellar restaurant. A saxophonist was giving a special performance that evening, and we were invited back. Why not? We couldn't think of a better way to end the trip!

As the restaurant filled up, we began to feel that there was something very special about to happen. My traveling companion looked at me, and I had to explain. I told her I wasn't sure what was up, but I had a feeling she'd be dancing on the tables before the night was over. That wasn't the half of it.

The guests at the restaurant sat at benches, picnic-style. It was friendly and warm. Everyone felt like family. As the evening progressed and we became more enchanted with the music and atmosphere, we played our own makeshift musical instruments and eventually ended up (yes, you guessed it) dancing on the tables. By the time the party was over, we only had a few hours until we needed to leave for the airport, and one of our new friends from the restaurant had offered to take us. It was the perfect end to a life-altering trip.

We arrived in New York the day before the Fourth of July. I felt like Dorothy in the Wizard of Oz. "There's no place like home." It is wonderful to explore the world, and ultimately, it makes you appreciate home and all the meaning that holds so much more. We had learned so much in just a few short weeks.

The desire was gone to attempt to beat the universe into submission, in an effort to force our version of the plan on a situation. In fact, we had pretty much let go of the planning thing altogether. If something didn't appear to be happening according to plan, we were content (albeit curious) to see what Spirit had in store for us. It was so much more fun to let the adventure unfold.

We knew that we could go out the door thinking that we were on our way to someplace in particular, and there was an excellent chance we would end up someplace entirely different. We were content with the experience that manifested. We were free! Life would never be the same.

"All it takes is a little teamwork."

Don't get me wrong, though. It's not about giving up responsibility for your life, only about allowing room for higher guidance. If you've been meditating for a while, you know how it feels to enter the void where this happens. You are actually the observer in your meditation.

If I could get to this place every time I meditate, I would have the anticipation of a child at the gates of Disneyland. Any question I ask is answered instantly. There is no doubt that the answer received emerges from the place in me that knows my highest truth. My ego is set aside. In fact, I can see how it affects my life.

When this happens, I have the sensation that my head is floating independently from my body. I can look down at myself sitting in meditation; it's an out-of-body experience. This place is permeated with magick. Miracles are ordinary events. I come out of meditation awestruck.

I actually *was* my super-conscious. I know it's there, and there is a plan. I have assumed the role of designated driver, but I am not alone. The navigator sits in the passenger seat, ready to assist me as long as I am not too stubborn to accept help. The navigator has every map, with all the sections of detail to direct me to just where I need to be.

Sometimes I want to pull over and just let the navigator drive. Wouldn't that be much easier? It doesn't work that way, and ultimately, we wouldn't be happy. We want the control. The navigator can tell us where we're going, where we need to turn next, but we have to actually make the turn.

I'm sure you've been on a road trip and have assumed the role of driver or navigator. If you are not in tune with each other and don't work as a team, you end up missing exits and turns. You can drive around in circles, trying to get your bearings.

If you work together, you give each other what is needed to successfully reach your destination. The driver says, "I just saw a sign that could mean we need to turn soon. What do you think?" The navigator consults the map and confirms that indeed this is the proper place to turn. If the navigator has a good relationship with the driver, he could offer additional information. "You need to turn right here and, about a mile further, you will need to take a left." The driver then chooses a lane that is appropriate for a left turn.

This is the way your life will be, if you develop a strong relationship with your guide or guides. Your life is one road trip after another, but you're never alone. You can rely on your guides to help you make the most of your journey.

"Seeing is believing."

When you ask for what you desire to manifest, ask for exactly what you want or something better, adding the reminder that it be attracted into your life 'under grace in a perfect way'. Using those few extra words, 'or something better', implies to your subconscious and the universe that you are open-minded about the outcome or detached from the exact result.

When you begin to see signs that the energy is moving, ask yourself, *"Is this what I wanted or better?"* If not, then keep working on it. The universe is just showing you that what you are doing is making a difference. You don't have to settle for scraps. You just need to be willing to persist until you reach your goal, without forcing your exact plan to fruition.

This is a great time to review your goals and affirmations. Do they still represent who you are becoming? Have your actions been consistently moving you towards where you say you want to go? Maybe you haven't manifested the big desire because you've been sending the universe mixed messages about what you want to create in your life. When you clean up your act, the big demonstration may well be just around the corner.

If, in reviewing your goals, you notice that several of them have had no activity, it's time to reevaluate. Is this really something you want to focus on this year? Maybe you need to eliminate it and channel your energy. You could put your energy into only doing the things that are easy and comfortable for you. You could focus all your energy on one or two goals. You'll start to see a pattern like this develop as you execute your plan. Whatever lacks energy will fall away. The fewer goals you have, the more time and energy you'll have to work on them.

I am one of those people that is capable of keeping many balls in the air. Just when I'm doing a pretty good juggling act, I'll take on another 'ball' and throw everything out of alignment. When I look at my goals, I have to realistically evaluate my ability to move everything forward simultaneously. If I have too many priorities, nothing comes to completion. I have to ask myself which goals I want to focus on. It requires energy and commitment to pursue each one.

"The first step is the hardest."

There have been many times when I have recognized that I was trying to control a situation, yet I didn't know quite how to let it go. Detachment was a very familiar term, but living it was another story. What could I do to occupy myself and send a clear message to the universe that I wasn't going to do anything until receiving further instructions?

You have probably gathered that I don't spend much time watching television. Now, in theory, this would be the perfect activity. The universe (and my subconscious) knows that I consider watching television to be a gross waste of time in most instances. I have never been a 'couch potato', and it would be a real stretch to relax and really let go of whatever had me worked up sitting in front of a television.

I discovered something else that works the same way; I can go to the movies. I love a great story and am inspired by the creativity that goes into creating a full-length feature film. Since what I am really lacking at these times is the connection to the more creative side of my brain, going to the movies actually seems to reconnect some loose wires. A couple of hours later, I emerge with a new perspective. My attitude has been effectively adjusted.

Going to the movies allows me to get out of my own way and quit the process of trying to force a solution to present itself. *"Spirit, you deal with it. In a few hours, I'll check back in and see if you're ready for me to move forward. I assume that, if you are, you'll have clear instructions prepared for me and they will be made available without stress and strain."* This approach has worked so well that I can't believe I spent so many years thinking I needed to continue forcing my way to a solution. I made it so much harder than it had to be.

Your activity might be something other than going to the movies. Remember, you need to be able to get away from everything. Taking a walk doesn't really help, because you are still in thinking mode. Whatever activity you choose, it should fully occupy your conscious mind and inspire creativity.

"Patience is a virtue."

Most people would say that patience is not their strongest virtue. I would be one of them. Patience is the hardest thing for me to practice, but 'doing nothing' is actually doing something very important. If you have asked for a definitive lead and you don't feel that you have been given clear direction, you need to sit still. The universe is working on it. Getting in the middle of things and stirring the pot will certainly make matters worse. More than likely, you will significantly delay the outcome that is being created.

If you reach the intended state of mind, you will be at peace. You will know that you can't miss a phone call you were meant to receive. You'll trust that the universe is in your corner and working on your problem, as if it had nothing better to do. The truth is, it doesn't. Universal resources aren't limited.

When you use the resources that have been divinely set aside for you, there is no need to concern yourself that you are taking resources that might have been allocated to someone else. The abundance of the universe is so great that it is a travesty to live a limited life. All you need to do is claim what is yours, wishing for no harm to come to another.

When you have come to the 'right' conclusion, you will know it if you've developed your self-knowledge. You will feel it in the place that is your center. As you begin to execute the plan based on the conclusion that was reached, things will fall into place. It will be relatively easy, usually much easier than you could have imagined.

Of course, *you* don't really come to the right conclusion. The right conclusion comes to you. You prepare yourself to receive it in whatever way works for you. For me, it's going to the movies; for you, it might be playing hockey. In that space of pure, unbridled creativity that has been primed with the request for guidance, the next move is given to you.

Sometimes it seems so easy that we doubt its authenticity. *"Why didn't I think of that?"* Actually you did, and at the perfect time. You couldn't have come up with it a moment sooner, without threatening the very precision of the universe.

"Timing is everything."

So when you really feel like you've done your part and what you've asked for doesn't manifest, it comes down to timing. There's something still blocking the energy flow. It helps to remind yourself of all the components that the universe must line up in order to manifest your desire.

I believe you literally could discover that your desire has already been made real in your life on some level, but as humans we want to see it progress step by step. You've seen how quickly it becomes real when you believe it is an easy request. There is no denying, then, that you are the one who ultimately decides how complicated or difficult things will be. But it can't always be easy. You're here to learn and grow. If you skipped the process, you wouldn't really be accomplishing anything.

The planets also influence the 'right' timing for emphasizing certain departments of your life over others. As they transit through the sky, they make aspects to your unique astrological makeup and generate energy that results in thoughts. So if you start feeling like you want to overhaul your life, you can study the energy that is influencing you and learn to use it constructively.

Have you ever gotten a couple of hours into your day and realized that you should have just stayed in bed? If we had to live like this all the time, life wouldn't be much fun. Nothing seems to work. There is something heavy in the air, and you're just agitated.

I have found it very interesting to mention this feeling to other people when it strikes me. It isn't just me feeling like this. There is an energy field that hangs over everyone's head. This tells you there's a good chance it has something to do with the planets.

On a day like this, my energy level is very low. I'm more sensitive and have a really short fuse. In my old life, I would grind through a day like this, making mistakes and feeling exhausted at the end of it.

When I recognize this feeling now, I give myself some space. I've already learned that trying to force myself to be highly productive will only result in messes I need to spend most of the next day cleaning up. Since anything I would force myself to do would certainly not produce great results, why do it?

It has never failed me. The next day, I wake up and the blanket has lifted. Whatever it was has moved through, and I can get back to the plan. Having given myself the space to move slowly and deliberately, doing only what absolutely had to be done, I can use the energy of this new day constructively. I am working in cooperation with the universe and flowing with the energy, rather than trying to swim upstream.

This same philosophy applies on a larger scale as well. There are probably areas of your life that need to be overhauled at any given time. Without proper direction, there's a good chance you could spend the energy in ways that are not productive or that you wouldn't consciously choose. In essence, the planets create the timing, and this can be manipulated to a certain degree, if you understand how the energy is attempting to assist you. You work in cooperation with it, rather than fighting the process.

"Don't go through life, grow through life."

I have gone through several periods in my life where I held on to the old, familiar life I had, even when I knew things needed to change. This resistance, in effect, created a dam of universal energy that could only be held at bay so long. When the dam broke, I was swept away in a flood of changes that left me clinging to a branch of my former life.

In these periods, change was not gentle. This was no stream created by a spring rain. In the desert, summer storms can be very dangerous. The ground has been baked by the sun, and water runs off as if it hit rock. The water collects quickly and floods to the lowest point, taking anything that isn't permanently attached with it.

This is what happens when you resist change. In essence, you are baking the ground. If you had planted seeds and embraced change incrementally, the rain would have been welcome. Instead, you are ripped free from your comfort zone and are forced to change, kicking and screaming, if that's how you choose for it to happen.

When you hold on to people, places, and things in your life that aren't working, everyone affected is unhappy and discontent. You might think that letting go of what isn't working will make you more unhappy and discontent than you are now. That actually might be momentarily true, but you have to make space in your life for what will work and what you say you want to create.

Think of the energy that is consumed when you are involved in activities you aren't committed to. Every moment spent on them drains you. When you are actively involved in activities that are supporting you in creating your life as you have dreamed it to be, you are energized. If you take a look at your action plan and all the things you need to do to execute it, you will realize that you don't have time for draining activities. You need to get on with it!

What you are holding onto is nothing more than a distraction that keeps you in the cage. You're the hamster going round and round on the wheel. The hamster might not have an opportunity to break free from its limited surroundings, but you do.

As you learn and grow, there is no question that your path will take off in a different direction. Sometimes, it will be only slightly altered. Other times, you will do an about-face. You can't really expect that everything and everyone that worked in your life on the old path will still be functional on the new one. That is a bit unrealistic.

Relationships are difficult because people change. When those changes affect the people involved in a way that make them incompatible, then something has to give. You either have to be willing to make enormous compromises or be willing to let go.

You have to be true to yourself. Are the compromises you're considering making consistent with the 'you' that you are becoming? If you compromise in a way that makes you less than you are, it won't work long-term. You might be able to buy some time, but you can only repress the 'you' that is shedding its skin for so long.

You can't really control growth. If you are reading this book, you have already waded in too far to turn back. The snake sheds its skin and feels exposed for a little while, until it weathers. Give yourself a little time to get comfortable in your new skin, and watch what wonders you attract from the universe.

When you choose happiness for yourself and take the action necessary to move in that direction, the universe will support you. Even if your choices affect other people and seem to create unhappiness in their lives, know that the most loving thing you can do for everyone is to take care of yourself. When you have done that, everyone you come in contact with will benefit.

Chapter 10

It's Perfect the Way It Is

"Go with the flow."

When you move quickly to looking for the opportunity in every challenging situation, you take a tremendous leap forward towards the perfect solution. You have to trust that the solution is already part of the plan. All you have to do is find it. *"What's next, Spirit? What do I need to learn or do to move through this situation quickly?"*

So what do you do when you trust that it's perfect, but right now, you are sitting in the midst of chaos and confusion? You give Spirit a wide berth and pray a lot. Your faith is being tested. When you are doing your work and feel that you are on the right path, it's just a waiting game.

To help keep things in perspective, I always start my prayers with: *"I expect and claim my divine guidance and inspiration. The universal intelligence that pervades all of creation is now permeating my entire life, and I am grateful."* As I listen to myself recite that prayer, I am reminded that my life is infused with universal intelligence. The perfection will appear as soon as you believe it will. This is the most difficult stage in the problem-solving process.

You are challenged to demonstrate your fearless faith and trust in the universe. *"Spirit, I can certainly come up with some pretty far-fetched ways you could solve this problem. What that basically tells me is that the solution will be a miracle."* Interesting, isn't it? It sounds so matter of fact. Expect a miracle. Why not?

You've certainly claimed miracles before. Now would be yet another really good time to prove that the universe is taking care of you. Break out your tool chest and go to work. Write through your own limited beliefs and generate possible solutions. Ask yourself why this is happening and see if you can move to the learning and growth available to you. Take a walk and connect with the miracles present in nature. Meditate yourself to a peaceful state of mind. Bless everything you can think to bless, including the current situation. Then let it go.

Until you are led to your next move, do nothing. Remember doing nothing *is* doing something. Someplace in the universe, everything that is going to happen has already happened. The plan is unfolding on many levels. The universe has no limits. The power is waiting to be tapped. Drawing on these concepts that we know to be true, it is easy to turn things over to this awesome intelligence.

In my college days, a group of my friends would head to Laughlin, Nevada, in the summer to float in the river. We used inner tubes and tied them together so that we would stay in a group.

Laughlin is a town a couple of hours away from Las Vegas that sits on the Colorado River. There are hotel-casinos every so often along the riverbank, and each one of them has a dock for the ferry that takes people from place to place. We knew to steer clear of the docks because the currents were treacherous if you got too close.

Well, we were having fun and not paying enough attention, and the next thing we knew we were being sucked into the current that was swirling around the dock. Several of us, including myself, were pulled under, and panic ensued. I can remember clearly being underwater and swimming as fast as I could to try to combat the current. I wasn't getting anywhere and knew that I would drown if I didn't do something different.

In a flash, I knew I just needed to stop and go with the flow. When I did, I spit out beyond the dock, and everyone that was on the surface was staring at me in amazement. I wasn't the only one that had lost my inner tube. The scene was pandemonium — overturned coolers with drinks floating everywhere.

One of our friends had a boat and began the recovery process. Before you knew it, we were all settled back in and floating peacefully.

When I talk about going with the flow, it is difficult for me not to come back to this experience. For me, it was life and death. If I hadn't stopped fighting and let the current take me where I needed to go, I wouldn't be here writing this book. Think of the energy I was wasting trying to fight the current. Going with the flow was effortless. Thank God I was paying attention. Even in a dire situation, I was capable of listening to and following instructions. All those lessons in school had paid off.

"Virtue is its own reward."

The perfection of the universe is demonstrated in its seeming imperfection. For people who use astrology to help them manage their lives, retrograde planets generally represent trying times. When a planet is retrograde, the energy is encouraging us to look behind the scenes, to pick up the covers and throw some light on things. Being that most of us are spread a little too thin already, we don't want to take the time to pay extra attention.

Since Mercury goes retrograde several times each year, it is the planet that causes the most concern. Mercury is the planet governing communication of all kinds — e-mail, FAX, snail mail, contracts. The list goes on. Because of our daily time pressures, we would rather avoid communications during these times than use the retrograde energy as intended.

When I can't get through to someone on the phone, for example, I trust that I need to rethink what I wanted to say to that person. When an e-mail gets lost in the black hole of Internet wasteland, I trust that the person receiving it would have misunderstood my message so it would have done more harm than good. (Speaking of all those lost e-mails, where <u>do</u> they go?)

Mercury retrograde, or any similar energy, provides us with an opportunity to pour over the details. Delays work to our benefit. When the planet's energy comes out of retrograde motion and goes direct, we are ready to proceed full steam ahead, having taken the time to prepare thoroughly. What seemed imperfect in the universe's plan was once again perfect; it was exactly what was needed.

A couple of months after I sold the accounting firm, I decided to take a ski vacation in Colorado. Since I was unemployed, I wanted to drive so that I would have the freedom to stay as long as I wanted to. One of my friends loves to ski, and she decided to join me on the trip. Her plan was to fly home when she needed to get back to work. We both have friends in the ski town we planned on visiting, so we had places to stay and were welcome.

It was the day before New Year's Eve, and we started our journey fairly early, hoping to arrive at our destination at a reasonable hour. The trip was going along smoothly, and we were beginning to look forward to dinner at our favorite sushi restaurant. We were about three hours away!

We were in my SUV and were sharing the driving duties. When we were about an hour west of Grand Junction, it was dusk. My friend was behind the wheel, and we were coming out of a big curve. I said anxiously, "What's that in the road?" There wasn't much light, and it was difficult to make out. The only thing to do was try to maneuver around it, at 80 miles per hour.

The minute my friend pulled the wheel, she lost control of the vehicle. We began to swerve all over the road, out of control. My last conscious memory is of seeing the guardrail approaching head on.

The next thing I knew, the vehicle was laying on its side in the middle of the highway. My friend was dangling above my head by her seat belt. After assessing the situation (there was no blood), I said, "We're in the middle of the highway. We have to get out of this car!" Without thinking, she released her seatbelt and fell on me. We tried to open the door, but it was too heavy since we had to push it up.

By this time, other vehicles were stopping to help us, and a couple of men managed to get the door open. A trucker stopped to put out flares. A family stopped and gave us blankets because we were standing on the side of the highway, in the middle of winter, with no coats.

It took quite a while, but the highway patrol finally arrived. The trooper put us in the back of the patrol car to warm up while he investigated the accident scene. The culprit was a lawn chair in the middle of the road. In hindsight, we might have just driven over it, but we could have blown a tire and met the same or worse fate.

In the patrol car, I was calling the rental car companies in Grand Junction, trying to figure out how we would get to where we were going. I can assure you neither one of us was too keen on getting behind the wheel of a car so when the car rental wasn't working out, we didn't push it.

The officer called the tow company, and they brought a flatbed to put what was left of my vehicle on. There wasn't an angle that you could look at that hadn't been pretty much demolished. It was hard to believe that neither one of us had been injured. We got out to supervise the clean-up and found that our skis (in the rack) had come off the roof and slid down the highway. They didn't have a scratch on them.

We got back in the patrol car, and the officer drove us to the Grand Junction airport. I was in charge of figuring out how we were going to continue our journey, while my friend was responsible for waiting for the tow truck. The officer asked the drivers to follow us to the airport so that we could get all of our things out of the car.

I went into the airport and confirmed that there were no flights that would serve our purpose. We had already exhausted the rental car idea. I walked back out to the curb and saw a shuttle van approaching. I flagged the driver down and asked him if by chance he could take us where we needed to go.

By this time, the flatbed had shown up, and my friend was working with the drivers to recover our things. I directed the shuttle driver's attention to the mangled mess that was my SUV and explained my problem. He said he couldn't take us because his passengers were headed to a different destination, but he had an idea. We walked inside the airport, and he made a phone call to his wife. He asked her to bring their other van and take us where we needed to go. I thanked him and went back to help my friend, who was still working with the tow truck drivers.

There were several things that had ended up on the floorboard, amidst the broken glass, that were very hard to recover in the dark. The drivers certainly went above and beyond the call of duty trying to help us. We all knew that we would probably never see this vehicle again.

At one point, they asked us how we got the officer to bring us to the airport. We looked puzzled. Don't they do that for everyone in this kind of situation? They also said that they wouldn't normally have brought our vehicle to the airport. They only had because the officer had instructed them to.

We were still missing a couple of things but finally had to give up the search. Our van had arrived. The driver packed us up, and we were back on the road. She even offered to stop so we could get something to eat, since our sushi dinner was obviously out of the question by now. When we finally showed up at my friend's house and shared the entire experience, he was amazed that we didn't have a scratch on us. Nothing less than a miracle.

We woke up the next morning and felt like celebrating life. Sure we should have been resting, but we wanted to take advantage of every moment.

I did some soul-searching for the next several days (and months). Why did this happen? I know that the accident was part of a perfect plan, even if I still don't fully understand what that plan was or is.

I do know that, through this experience, I saw just how much I'd grown. Just after the accident, my friend said to me, "I'm so sorry. I ruined our vacation. I wrecked your car." I told her it could have happened just as easily to me and that we should celebrate that we were alive.

I also know that I learned more in those few hours than I learned in several years of intense study. I watched as the universe provided everything we needed and took delicate care of us. The only injury either one of us sustained (besides sore necks) was a bruise on my shin. Miraculously, it was just above the top of my ski boot so it didn't interfere with skiing.

Then, there were all the people that went out of their way to help us that day, something I remind myself of whenever I see violence and cruelty in the world. Most importantly, I no longer have a fear of death because, when I saw the guardrail coming at me, I left my body. As a result, I know I can check out whenever I need to.

All in all, I saw how we really didn't lose anything, down to still being able to ski the next day. In fact, we gained so much. The universe supports me every day in every way, and the accident was the perfect stage for that point to be made.

"Persistence wears down resistance."

To really own this universal potential, you have to accept that there are multiple levels of yourself at work simultaneously. Your higher self or super-conscious is in essence your God-self. It sits in the skybox with the perfect vantage point. It's easy to be a good coach with this perspective, right?

So all you really have to do is own that part of yourself. You are all that you can imagine and more. You already know your soul's plan and are doing what you need to be doing in this moment to get you where you need to be next so that you will be doing exactly what you need to be doing in that moment to get you where you need to be after that. As you can see, this could go on and on, but by now you get the picture.

It's about taking personal responsibility for creating your life. And if God is within you, then how could anything you create be less than perfect? The universe isn't doing to you; you are doing to yourself.

At first, this can cause a heck of a lot of anxiety. "Why would I do this to myself? Good grief! I know better than this." But, if you trust that your super-conscious higher self has a plan that is currently being implemented, then it should be fairly easy to trust that your subconscious might be what is throwing a wrench into the plan, causing delays and detours.

Acknowledging this is the first step to taking its power away. You need to recognize that it is capable of sabotage. That shouldn't be too tough since you don't have to look far to see where you've come close to reaching a goal and then done something that set you way back. It was like playing Monopoly, "Go directly to jail. Do not pass go. Do not collect $200."

You know that you wouldn't consciously have spoiled things and have a feeling that something is at work in the situation that doesn't seem to have your best interest in mind. As you begin to understand why your subconscious does what it does, you see how, in fact, it does think it is working in your best interest. It is in heightened defense mode, protecting the known and comfortable.

Once you understand it, you can begin to give it what it needs to feel comfortable moving from what was known and comfortable to a new version of that. Sometimes it's just a few bug fixes to the program, and other times you need a whole new version. The good news is that it can be fixed and it can happen overnight once you see where the problem is.

Go back and remind yourself. *"I am doing what I need to be doing in this moment to get me where I need to be next* so that I will be doing exactly what I need to be doing in that moment to get me to where I need to be after that." It doesn't get more perpetually perfect than that.

That's not to say it's always easy to deal with. For a perfectionist like myself, it's sometimes a stretch to really embrace the perfection of the universe, when it appears on the surface to be quite flawed. Each of us can have different issues with accepting the universe's version of perfection, and some of that can relate to our astrological make-up.

In astrology, the sun sign is the one most talked about. While it is an important component of your astrological make-up, in no way does it even begin to capture your real essence or what makes you tick. This is easily demonstrated by taking a look at my make-up.

I'm pretty much of a perfectionist, which relates most closely to Virgo energy. Virgo is the zodiac's perfectionist. While Virgo is not my sun sign, I have tons of Virgo energy in my chart. For the technicians, I have a stellium in Virgo in the first house. As a result, I can make myself sick trying to micromanage things to ensure perfection.

The problem for a perfectionism-afflicted person isn't in striving for perfection. That's a good thing that everyone should embody. The problem is that the perfectionist is never satisfied. We try to go places you can't get to. To compound the problem, we have an extremely difficult time choosing our battles. *Everything* needs to be perfect. From the smallest detail to the broad brushstroke, we will pick, pick, pick, until we finally give up. "It has to be good enough."

As I have gotten to know myself better, I have learned to let things go. I look at a situation and ask myself if it is really something that I need to work over until it gets as near to perfection as I can humanly get. I have learned to accept people just as they are, seeing the perfection in each person's approach to life. In other words, I am using my Virgo energy to be of service rather than to pick things apart. This ultimately results in self-acceptance, which is the most loving thing we can do for the universe.

"Better late than never."

When I embarked on this journey, my biggest concern was that I wouldn't be able to exist in the world that was familiar to me. I knew things had to change so I was willing to risk it, but it was scary. I was living solely from one side of my brain and saw little value in what the other side might add if I tapped into its potential.

The spiritual world seemed very abstract to me. I lived life with both feet firmly planted on the ground, and I was naïve enough to think it was working. Whenever I encountered a problem, I would sit down and go through it logically, forcing my way to a solution.

It blows me away to retrace my steps and remind myself of how far I've come. Who was that person? The other day, I was faced with a problem that needed attention. I immediately approached it from a spiritual perspective. There was no thought process of, "Which method do I use?" It was automatic.

Something triggered a past memory, and I was jolted by the realization that I am much more comfortable in my spiritual approach to problem-solving than I ever was using logic. The spiritual world that, not so long ago, seemed so abstract is now where

I choose to firmly plant my feet. The guidance I receive from a powerful meditation is much more trustworthy than my pros and cons approach. I live a balanced life now, using both sides of my brain in an interdependency that makes the world a brighter place.

As you get comfortable working with this approach to problem-solving, you won't want to waste any time. *"Let's get on with it."* Time and time again, you've been shown how perfectly everything falls into place eventually. You will want to do everything you can to facilitate the process.

"Only love is real."

As you create yourself as you aspire to be, you are in essence traveling down the aisles of the universe's supermarket. "I'll take one of those." You pick something up and take a look at the label. If it's full of sugar (or anything not healthy), you put it back. For the most part, you select staples, with a splurge here and there.

When it's time to go through the checkout stand, you mentally go back over your list. "Did I get everything I came to get?" You'll probably find you actually added a few things you didn't know you needed before you got there. You head home with lots to work with.

Fortunately, once the supply is depleted, you'll be ready to go back and explore some new territory, aisles you never knew existed before. This is the universe's supermarket; it is infinite and pure potential.

The work you do to further your knowledge of yourself lifts the veil from the illusion that you are separate and that your actions are independent from others. What you do affects everyone. We are all one, big, extended, functionally-dysfunctional family. We see characteristics and traits in others that we embrace as personal aspirations. And, in contrast, we also turn away from the characteristics and traits that we don't like to admit we embody. At times, this even manifests as intolerance or, beyond that, violence.

People beginning their journey of self-discovery often ask, "If the universe knows only perfection, how can there be violence and intolerance? How can that be perfect?" It is perfect in that it shows you in living color what your choices are. You can be this, or you can be that. The choice is yours.

It can all be changed with love. Love raises the vibration. When you unconditionally love yourself and the others around you, it makes everything easier to live with. Even if you choose not to live with something, you can accept it. It is a part of who you are; it is what's real. Real is what you feel and know inside, not what you see with your eyes. Perhaps that's why it has been written that only love is real.

Chapter 11

There Are No Problems

"There are no problems, only opportunities."

We live in an illusion. We are conditioned to see problems as just that, problems. They happen *to* us. We are victims of life and the ways of the world. It sounds good (or at least easy), but the illusion just doesn't hold water when you take a closer look.

There are countless stories of very successful people that are the 'product' of environmental circumstances that they could have used to play victim. Rather, they have risen above the challenges and used them as their own catalysts to greatness.

Our environment depends, in large part, on the characters we cast in our production before we embarked on this journey. So, if we say that we are a product of our environment and we have chosen that environment, then aren't we really the product of our own choices? We live in a fantasy world that we create, and it is more real than any concrete, dirt under our feet, or sand between our toes than we have experienced.

If you have gotten this far, you have already let go of the illusion and shifted your perception. You know there are many versions of reality, and you choose which version you will live within. When you outgrow your current version, you simply create a new one. You can do whatever you want to do. All you need is the determination and will.

It doesn't matter what you've aspired to in the past, you can always move further. The situations that appear in your life are the catalysts for that movement. They put things in motion, causing you to take action. How could you view them as problems? Without issues that rock your boat, you would have no reason to push yourself to be more today than you were yesterday. As thinking beings, we want (and need) to be challenged. Like the golfer, we are never quite satisfied until the ball lands within a foot of the cup.

"If at first you don't succeed, try, try again."

As you begin the process of learning anything that is new to you, you will certainly not be in your best form. You have to be willing to be bad before you can be good. You have to take the risk in order to move forward on your path.

When you choose to be a leader, you are by nature a risk taker and perhaps even a trendsetter. A leader has to be willing to pioneer the way, setting an example for those that fall in behind to follow.

I have been the proverbial 'Indian with the arrow in my back' many times in my life. At the accounting firm, I always seemed to be implementing an idea whose time had not quite come. At conferences, I would be ridiculed. "That will never work. I could never get the people at my firm to buy into that."

Fortunately for me, I didn't listen to them when they said it wouldn't work. In fact, I didn't wait to confer to try it. We went for it and put the commitment behind it. Two years later, everyone else was following along, doing what they earlier said couldn't be done.

That's not to say that you will always succeed when you take a risk. Keep in mind, though, that a failure is never lacking in value. In fact, failure can be invaluable. It is the failed experiment that produces the most ingenious inventions. After all, Post-it Notes were the result of a botched experiment making glue.

If you have been really honest and stretched yourself in setting your goals, no doubt you have challenged yourself to do something you have always wanted to do but never tried. In some way, the fear of being bad at it kept you from even getting started.

It is natural to experience fear when you are faced with change. You can't go through the process we've talked about in this book without making change your friend. This means that you must also bring fear into your camp. There it is again, that fear energy. *"How can I use it to move me forward?"* It is extremely powerful.

When my friend and I were being robbed on the train in Italy, it was fear that produced the super-human strength I used to strike back at our oppressor. You have to learn to recognize it and harness it, in order to be able to use it effectively.

Most of us feel fear and turn away from it. "That's too scary; I have too much to deal with to bring that home with me." The problem is that it follows you. Until you assume the position of power, fear is in control. Sooner or later, you will have to sit down with it and examine it. *"Where is it coming from?"*

Once you figure out what you're afraid of, ask yourself, *"What is the worst thing that could happen?"* The fear is generally much greater than the actual feared outcome. When you recognize that, you begin to take its power away. You can dissipate the power or transfer it. Feel the fear and do it any way. Use that fear to motivate yourself. Actors use the fear of stepping onto the stage to help them move into character. We are all actors in the starring role of our lives. The more you've prepared yourself by hanging out with your fear, the more powerful you'll feel.

No matter how bad things may seem in the moment, you know you always survive. Spirit shows us time and time again, that we are guided, protected, and provided for. Every time I have that demonstrated, I take a few moments to pull it in. As I do, hindsight becomes foresight. I know that before I have even asked, my request has been answered. I don't need to consume energy focusing on the problem. My energy goes into living and learning.

Once I've learned what I need to learn, the problem (which only existed for this purpose) disintegrates. The solution demonstrates itself, and I am on to the next adventure, pausing momentarily to reflect. *"Am I satisfied with the way I handled the last problem that I encountered?"* I know that my actions and reactions define me.

The universe (or actually your higher self) will send you another scene that gives you an opportunity to try out what you've learned. If you've said you aren't going to make the same mistake again, rest assured that the universe will present you with a cleverly disguised situation that tests your understanding. Are you aware enough to recognize it? Have you really healed the part of yourself that seems to need to keep going down that same bumpy road?

When you keep making the same mistakes, saying yes when you need to say no, there is a place within yourself (at a less than fully conscious level) that has a need that has not been met. Until that place inside has been brought into the light and is being satisfied in healthy ways, it will keep tugging at you to travel the same road, hoping for a different destination.

Of course, it doesn't work that way. You have to take a different road to end up in a different place. I have seen this at work in my life, and it is deflating. "How could I know that I need to take a different approach and still make the same mistake?" I even got to the point where I could see the bait being dangled in front of me, and I still took it.

The subconscious is so elusive. If there is a devil, the subconscious is it. In its desperation to preserve its current reality, it becomes your worthy opponent. And it knows all your weaknesses. You have to make your subconscious your friend. Bring the enemy into your camp, and find out what it needs. What is it that you most value? If you can see how making a specific choice will bring more of that into your life, then it's an easy sale.

It can really be quite simple. The problem can be solved in a moment of divine inspiration. By satisfying the subconscious need, you free yourself to make conscious choices that will lead you to your full potential.

"A calm sea does not make a skilled sailor."

The further along I move in this process, the longer the road seems. Just about the time I'm feeling like I have something figured out, I realize that I have just peeled one layer and exposed myself to how far I still have to go. You never really 'get there'. The more you know, the more you realize you don't know. It's just that the learnings aren't quite as profound or life-altering once you have the basic training under your belt. It becomes much more subtle. You have to look a little harder and be more alert.

With the pursuit of mastery come plateaus, where you are tempted to rest on the results of your prior efforts. This is a comfortable place until you are ready to ask, "What's next?" You will be sent exactly what you need to push you to the precipice. Another turning point: *"Do I take the leap of faith, or do I turn away and try to find satisfaction here on the plateau?"*

You might resist a little at first. "Look at all I've accomplished and learned. Can't I just enjoy it a little longer?" That's not what you came here for. Once you've achieved this year's goals, you will be a little stronger and wiser. From this place of confidence, you will boldly set next year's goals, knowing that you have more tools in your tool chest to help you reach them.

You are always within the process. Even on the plateau, you are learning. *"What is it like to live knowing what I have learned to this point? How am I different? What do I still need to work on?"* You learn something and integrate it with everything else you've put in your data banks.

Maybe this learning challenges a belief you have held. Then, you have to put some thought (and possibly study) into what belief you will hold going forward. *"If I understand this better, can the two beliefs, that at first seemed mutually exclusive, find a peaceful place to co-exist?"* Whenever I reach this point, I find that, by probing a little deeper, there are similarities and common threads that bridge the concepts, giving me a rich, new understanding to work with.

My former business partner and I had very different strengths and weaknesses. At times, we would both get frustrated by how the other person was approaching a situation that we were facing. Then I realized that some of the characteristics that bothered me most were products of the qualities that made him the perfect partner for me. We complimented each other very well. After that, I learned to love him and accept him just the way he is.

Our friendship and the relationship that we had built over the years helped us see how each person's approach actually benefited the whole. We used the strengths of each individual to make a greater sum of the parts. We had to accept that we both embodied weaknesses that, if acknowledged, could be minimized or even turned to our advantage.

You have to make room for options and compromise in order to build a relationship based on love, acceptance, and tolerance. *"My way is **a** way, not **the** way."* There are many roads that lead home, and they all offer their own benefits and advantages.

The world is full of teachers and students. At any given point in time, you assume either or both roles. While we have all had lots of teachers in our lives, some are more memorable than others. That's not to say we always appreciate our teachers when we're in the throws of learning.

Can you see how you've been a teacher to someone who may not have appreciated it at the time? When you're the student, have you chosen to appreciate the role your teacher is playing? Our parents, in particular, are catalysts in our soul development. They personify issues that we know we need to work on if we are to rise in consciousness and vibrate on a different level. That's why we chose them.

Many times, it is the teacher that the universe produces in a moment of need that has the most compelling impact on who you are and will be. When the student is ready, the teacher appears. Be grateful that your teachers have been willing to meet the challenge. You serve each other as your paths cross.

"Don't limit your challenges, challenge your limits."

There is a good chance that, as you sharpen your skills, you will be given more challenging material to work with. The adversity you experience tests your character. You get to see what you're made of. As a result, you challenge yourself to be a little better next time.

After taking several months to process the learning from my trip to Europe and working my way through another tax season, I realized it was time for me to consider the next adventure in my journey. I asked my friend, the same friend that accompanied me to Europe, if she was game for another jaunt. When she said she was interested, I told her she could pick the place since I had chosen Europe the previous year.

She had been thinking about a trip to Brazil that she had heard about and said that was what she wanted to do. To her surprise, I said, "Great. Get me the information and I'll put it together." A few months later, we were on our way to Rio.

At the time, I felt that I didn't really know who I was. If my name hadn't been on my American Express card and I didn't have a sense that the bill would be paid, I'd really have felt like no one. It wasn't that it was really lonely; I had companionship. I wasn't isolated; I was around people. It was a lack of identity. Now *that* was something to look for on this journey.

We were going to stay in a community near Rio. I had no idea what to expect since I didn't know the country, the people, or much about the spiritual practices that the community was organized around. I had already learned that I really couldn't talk about it; just about anyone I would try to share with would go directly into fear. "Brazil is dangerous. The people are not to be trusted." I could go on, but it really isn't worth the paper.

We took a bus from the Rio airport, riding in the front seats with a really lovely view. It felt like a perfect start to the next phase of the journey. I thought, "Maybe that's what this experience is supposed to feel like - having front row seats!"

There were lots of kids by the side of the road. I wondered if they were waiting for the school bus. School is such an interesting thing. Of course, everyone needs reading, spelling, writing, and math. Everything else is just an experiment, right?

I wondered if there was an easier way to find what makes music in your soul than to experiment for years. Wouldn't it be wonderful to be guided from an early age? That just feels right to me.

We arrived at our destination and were greeted warmly. We were part of a group of 20 or so people from North America that had come to join in the community's annual festivities and experience a spiritual journey.

We were shown to our room. We had been assigned a room in one of the nicer buildings on the property. I had a futon that was on a platform just off the ground. My friend had a mattress on the floor. With no linens, we used our sleeping bags. The window stayed open all the time. We shared our room with lizards and an enormous spider.

Rio was experiencing a draught, and since the community was dependent on rain for its water supply, the situation was critical. They had water trucked in for necessities only. People from our group had been assigned to homes all over the community. Several people that I became close to were staying at the top of the hill. Because of their location, they got the first cut of any rain water that accumulated, so they actually had a shower. I would pack a small bag and hike up 63 vertical steps to partake. The shower wasn't hot, but with an alternative of no shower at all, it was bliss.

Not long into this experience, I told my friend that I knew I wouldn't stay until the time of our planned departure. I knew I needed to stay until I had learned what I needed to learn, but I couldn't imagine that taking three weeks. And how long could I live in these conditions?

It didn't take long for my perspective to change. A week later, I wrote this in my journal: "The energy is so blissful. Love is all there is! Boy, have we grown! Last year, we were playing Truth and Drink in Brindisi. This year, same game, very different experience. Instead of terror on the train, it is love and friendship. Common interests."

"All the functions I go to in Las Vegas where no one speaks my language. I come to Brazil where the people speak Portuguese, and they're easier to understand. We hung around for hours last night just taking in every moment. What a contrast! At home, I tell everyone I have to go home because it's my bedtime. Really it's because I'm bored and I feel like I have very little in common with them."

"We are all so different now. We aren't the same people that arrived a week ago. We all died. I get it - the Shaman's death. Actually, I think we've died a few times. Happy, happy, more happy. Love, love, more love."

We spent another two weeks living and loving more fully than I had ever known possible. We came to love our meager surroundings and didn't miss any of what I thought home was. The creature comforts that I treasured at home were a distant second to the feeling of home that I was experiencing here.

By the time our journey came to an end, I was the one that wasn't ready to leave. I knew I needed to take what I had learned home with me and apply it to my life. I knew that I had changed in profound ways and that the only way to fully understand those changes was to go back to the life I had left behind several weeks before.

Again, I had learned so much. I knew at the core of my being that love is what truly matters. There really are no problems that love can't solve, resolve, or heal. All you need to do is ask, *"What would love do now?"* The answer will immediately shift your experience, given the opportunity.

"The journey is the destination."

As I strengthen my connection to the level of consciousness where we all merge, I find that I become more and more sensitive to the suffering of others. I don't want to witness violence or intolerance. It goes right to the core of my being.

Even a movie can spark this reaction. If I go to see a heavy drama, I am immobilized for days afterwards. People will say, "It's only a movie; it's not real. Can't you separate fantasy from reality?" The problem for me is that I know every story is based, in some part, on a true story.

Why would I want to spend time with darkness? It doesn't compute for me that people really seem to enjoy witnessing the pain of others. If there's something wrong with me because I don't find entertainment there, then I am content in my dysfunction. I want to focus on the possibilities and where we want to go.

I am very selective in choosing what will be allowed to attach itself to my programming. Like a computer virus that we unwittingly unleash, the culprit comes through the television or movie screen. It has its own agenda and is invested in moving its mission forward. If that agenda and mission are counter to your own, you need to steer clear. Focus on what you want your world to be like, and support that vision from every angle.

In this accomplishment-driven world, it is sometimes easy to lose focus on what is really important. While you are busy getting things done, it is easy to lose sight of why you're really doing it. When I feel the anxiety building (so much to do and a limited amount of time to do it), I have to remind myself that it's not what I do but how I do it that defines me. It's the journey that makes the destination (when reached) that much sweeter.

You can't fool yourself. You know in your heart, subconscious, or super-conscious, that your intent is pure. As you work with the concepts in this book, you will accumulate knowledge. The most important of this knowledge is that of self.

The better you know yourself, the easier will be your journey. Changes you want to make can be made effortlessly because you have the tools to understand what has kept you in your current behavior pattern. You have a genuine love of self because you understand what motivates you and invokes emotion. You know your current self and all the selves you've been in the past. You know where you're going and celebrate your progress.

Self-knowledge is cumulative. You have a history, and rather than making you a victim, it empowers you.

Accepting that what's important is the journey, and the process that goes along with it, forces you to look at how you've accomplished something, rather than just that you got there. If the sacrifices that had to be made outweigh the end result, have you really made progress?

Life begs for balance to be whole. The pendulum swings in a wide arc as you scatter your energies in many different directions. When it begins to settle somewhere near the middle, you have found the place where true wholeness lies. Whatever you accomplish from this space will undoubtedly enhance your life.

Chapter 12

A Bit of Ancient Wisdom

"Tune in and turn on."

We are living in a time where science is no longer the answer to all our problems. Science itself has admitted that its theory that everything is observable and measurable doesn't describe the world in which we live. Many scientists have shared that their greatest breakthroughs came about after they stopped trying to solve a problem analytically. The analytical mind is loaded with data about a problem. The intuitive mind processes the information in a completely different way, allowing you to see new creative solutions.

Solving problems creatively is not a new idea. In fact, it seems an underlying factor in all of nature. In the theory of evolution, problem-solving is seen as the primal activity to address the primal challenge of survival. In animals, trial solutions to problems exhibit themselves in the form of new reactions or behaviors. If the new ways of being work, then the creature incorporates the learning into its very anatomy.

Humans function quite similarly. As we identify problems in our lives and accept that our current way of being has contributed to creating them, we try new ways of being. If we are successful in altering our circumstances, we incorporate the learning at a very deep soul level. Problem-solving is our way to soul development.

In the search for answers, we have found new ways of dealing with both our world and ourselves, and we have rediscovered traditional methods of healing and self-development. These typically fall under the umbrella of metaphysics. Metaphysics is a branch of philosophy that deals with non-material, spiritual causes. It was an accepted branch of science for most of our history.

Many metaphysically-minded people believe that there is a cosmic database known as the Akashic records. These records are thought to include all knowledge of the world – past, present, and future. They exist on the spiritual plane and can be accessed through processes like meditation. It is believed that Edgar Cayce, who offered some of the most insightful and healing readings of the century, was able to do so by accessing these records. Others, like Carl Jung, describe it as a collective unconscious.

Through meditation, you can tap into that realm and hear not only your own intuitive self but also the thoughts of others.

This type of psychic information has formed much of the basis for what is today considered 'new' spirituality. This channeled wisdom is based on the concept that we all possess the truth within our own selves and that we simply have to seek guidance from that place. A true master won't tell you to follow a specific teaching, but rather will encourage you to develop yourself to the point of discerning your own truth.

Psychic ability is as old as civilization itself. It allows you to access information about the past, present, and future, in a way that cannot be explained using the known laws of nature. This ability is basically a right-brain function. The right hemisphere of the brain is the intuitive, creative side that processes information holistically.

Our culture emphasizes left-brain thinking over right-brain thinking. Over time, this emphasis limits your access to your creative potential. In ancient times, people were more willing to trust their intuition and to look for answers from within.

Still, everyone has some degree of psychic ability. The process of developing that ability is entwined with the process of spiritual development. As you develop your intuitive abilities and stretch the muscles in your right brain, you begin to integrate both ways of knowing. As you gain insight into yourself, you know what your path is and where that is leading you. You access your own deep wisdom and use it logically to make choices and solve problems in your life.

"Be all that you can be."

Much of the ancient wisdom available to us has been passed on through time by courageous and enlightened souls. Those entrusted with the knowledge in ancient times passed it along, often secretly and at great risk to their own lives. Fortunately for those of us who choose to access it, these teachers for all of time were willing to make this effort and take the associated risks.

Like many others, Confucius, one of the great figures in the history of human thought, did not consider himself the author of what he taught, but rather an heir and transmitter of ancient learning developed over the course of many centuries. As a philosopher and teacher, his sayings, which have been preserved and studied over thousands of years, addressed core human issues.

Confucius expected people to do their own thinking, and his thought-provoking words were designed to stimulate this. He believed that the moral foundation of social order rested on humanity that required, in his view, knowledge. Knowledge leads to self-improvement, and, by improving ourselves, we improve others.

Once you embrace the process of self-development, you begin to see the benefits of tapping into ancient wisdom to help guide your course. Even though you may not be able to explain how you tap into this wisdom or where it comes from, you can still benefit from it. One explanation that helps synthesize this concept relates to our states of consciousness.

It is widely accepted that there are several levels of consciousness. The conscious mind is at the physical level and manifests through the senses. The subconscious stores impressions from the conscious mind and picks up far more than we can conceive of. The super-conscious mind is the original spiritual pattern. Man's development depends on his ability to release spiritual energy from this higher area of the unconscious and bring it into conscious expression.

Edgar Cayce, often referred to as the 'sleeping prophet', was never consciously aware of anything he said during his readings. He was functioning at an unconscious level. Much of the information that came through him was not consciously known by the individual who asked for his help. Psychologists admit that establishing communication between two unconscious minds, based on desire and permission, can provide useful information in solving problems.

As a result of his work, Cayce described the soul as an arrangement of energy made up of spirit, mind, and will. The spirit is the essence of life force; the mind is the creative building quality; the will is the power of choice. He believed that, within every being, there is a force that seeks to constantly move toward God. Beyond achieving physical success, a person has the power to choose the way that will mean a step forward along the path in his spiritual progress. By making an effort, the next step is opened to him from within. The search for God may use any condition, barrier, or problem as a stepping stone for further spiritual growth. Cayce's readings continually stress positive thought and action, in which one holds the mind to constructive activity and exercises free will.

Free will is an important concept in self-development. Any form of divination, from astrology to tarot, provides input on your path, given the direction you are heading at the time. It does not mean that where you are going now is where you will inevitably end up. Instead, it gives you insight you can use to help you determine if you need to alter your course to end up where you really want to be. For example, with astrology, simply knowing the influences the planets have on you gives you the opportunity to decide how to work with those influences. You decide how you are affected and exercise your free will to change the course of events in your life.

"This too shall pass."

Astrology in the ancient world was the first serious scientific attempt to explore the limits of determinism and the predictive powers of an all-embracing cosmology. In a sense, it was the precursor of all subsequent scientific efforts at predicting celestial phenomena. Science is a particular way of investigating the natural world that involves collecting data, looking for patterns in the data collected, and consequently constructing conceptual models that lead to refined predictions based on the data studied.

Anyone who has even the most limited understanding of astrology can see that it has undeniably been approached throughout history as a science. Astrology is a well-ordered system of calculation that can be applied to objective criteria. It dates back 4,000 years to Babylonian civilizations. The movements of the planets and stars were charted as a way to understand the change of seasons and facilitate agriculture.

Socrates, Plato, Aristotle, and others had an important influence on the growth of the science of nature, particularly astronomy. They studied the planets and their motions, leading to the understanding we have today. These great Greek thinkers were mainly concerned with trying to understand the world around them. This developed into an interest in people and how they ought to think and behave.

The Greeks thought only God could be wise. Men, however, could be 'lovers of wisdom'. If individuals acted with right judgment and wisdom, they would think and behave appropriately. They could use the thirst for wisdom to fuel the search for the most general truths concerning the world in which we live.

As the study of the planets developed, the planetary cycles were connected to human and cultural events. Ancient astrologers believed that the planets had a direct influence on human events. The relationships between planets reflect the relationship of the individual to the universe.

There is a great deal of evidence that Earth's magnetic field and its many vibrations have effects on a very wide variety of living organisms, including humans. There is further evidence that the personalities of individuals are somehow related to the state of the solar system at the time of their births.

While it is still not fully understood, we do know that the solar system embodies a magnetic field that generates an associated electrical field. It is widely accepted that this field stimulates the central nervous system. We are inherently tuned in to this field, and it affects our thoughts and actions, ultimately creating our reality or life.

In essence, astrology allows people to understand the way they see the events that take place in their lives and, as a result, provides them with the ability to put these events in a perspective that makes them opportunities for growth. The information helps people understand who they are, what they are made of, and what behavior patterns manifest most strongly. With this information, life is easier to manage. Since an astrological reading requires that a great quantity of data be synthesized, most astrologers combine their psychic ability with their knowledge of data to interpret a person's chart.

Numerology is considered a sister science to astrology and dates back to Babylonia as well. In numerology, numbers are thought to represent qualities rather than just quantities. By analyzing the numerical values in your date of birth and full birth name, the numerologist can reveal the specific lessons that you seek to master in this lifetime.

In calculating the values, all sums are reduced to single-digit numbers ranging from one to nine. The patterns of energy that you will be dealing with in any specific year are determined by arriving at the sum total of your birth date and the current year, then reducing that number to a single digit. Each year of a nine-year cycle holds unique drives and motivations. In any given year of the cycle, the influences will be similar to those of the same year in previous and subsequent cycles. For example, in the fourth year of every nine-year cycle, numerology may indicate particularly strong influences relating to building your foundation. You will be drawn to activities that will help you do that. In a nine year, you will feel compelled to complete whatever has been left incomplete. If something hasn't been working in your life, you will feel the need to find resolution.

I was introduced to numerology seven years ago. At the time, I was under considerable stress and didn't feel like I had the time to take care of myself. All I wanted to do was crawl in a hole. There were mornings when I could barely pick my head up off the pillow. This was really scary for a person that was used to displaying super-human energy and accomplishing more in one day than most people accomplish in a week. A friend of mine was a surgeon, and I told him I thought I might have a brain tumor. In hindsight, this is comical, but at the time, I saw no humor in it.

When I had reached the lowest point, I discovered numerology and the work of Dusty Bunker. It turns out I was in a seven year. During that time period, my soul needed to recharge itself. The inward journey was the only agenda. The more I fought it, the worse I felt.

This understanding helped me to work with the energy. I could see that I was going through a phase. "This too shall pass." Since that time, I have made it a practice to consult numerology regularly. I use it in cooperation with my intense study of astrology.

"Play the hand you're dealt."

One of the most widely-used tools for divination is the tarot deck. It is believed that the cards first appeared in Italy in the fifteenth century. Over time, their origins were attributed to multiple ancient cultures, including those of Egypt and Israel. While none of the major archaeological findings supported any of these theories, what became apparent was the ability of tarot symbolism to cross all boundaries. Since then, tarot has been linked with nearly every religion or magickal system discovered to date. This tool, long considered a powerful forecaster of the future, is now viewed as timeless and as embodying significant knowledge that applies to every mystical path.

Over the years, the card images have gone through multiple incarnations that reflect the trends of the time yet do not impact the use of tarot as a tool. In any representation, the symbols and figures are metaphors for the soul's journey through life. Readers use the tarot deck as a channel for information that speaks to each person in an individual and intimate way.

An even more ancient method of divination is the use of rune stones. They date back to the time of the Vikings in Scandinavia. Late Scandinavian mythology tells us that the god Odin received the runes by hanging upside down on the tree of life. The rune's symbols are, in essence, an alphabet that can be used to foretell the future. They are read with specific regard to the symbolic meaning of the letters and also provide access to the reader's subconscious for insight into a problem or question.

The pendulum is considered one of the easiest and most effective tools for divination. Starting as early as 2000 B.C., pendulums were used by the priesthood as part of its mysticism. The pendulum is a tool that helps you gain clarity and empower your own sense of inner wisdom. It helps in accessing the super-conscious mind for guidance in choosing between different options. The basic premise is that the pendulum will help circumvent the subconscious and move the answer that is already within the super-conscious into the conscious realm.

Probably the earliest method of divination is the I Ching, or Book of Changes. The I Ching embodies Chinese folk wisdom and may go back as far as 3000 B.C. The system is based on 64 hexagrams that are made up of a block of six horizontal lines, either solid or broken.

The I Ching differs from other methods of divination in that it doesn't simply predict the outcome. It also recommends a course of action. It has come to be a blueprint for spiritual development, beyond its application in fortune-telling. As you understand the relationship that your individual actions have on the whole of life, right decisions can be made. The Book can also be used as a basis for study and helps the student understand the spiritual value of divination, providing key insights into their own personal growth.

"If it feels good, do it."

I make regular use of psychic readers specializing in all forms of divination – astrology, tarot, palm analysis, stones. A psychic will tell you about the future, as it relates to the present. This information should help you evaluate whether your current actions will have positive results in the future. You will either receive confirmation that you are on the right track or information that will help you redirect yourself. The reading gives you knowledge about yourself. In a way, it is similar to seeing a psychotherapist.

Whenever I enter the space for a reading, I prepare myself by praying. *"God, allow this person to be your messenger. I am prepared to hear what I need to hear at this moment. I am open to receive and trust that you will assist me in using the knowledge you have provided."* At this point, I have let go of my agenda. I rarely give a reader any specifics about what is concerning me in the moment. I only offer that I trust that they will share with me exactly what I need to know.

Most psychics bring themselves to an alpha state, the state of restful awareness between wakefulness and sleeping, to receive information for a reading. In reaching the alpha state, the right brain takes over from the left. Information that was previously inaccessible to the analytical portion of the mind, or the left brain, flows freely.

As we move through the reading, sometimes things will feel a little stuck. Without any information from me, the reader is in the difficult position of trying to synthesize what is being received into something meaningful. I might offer something that confirms that they are on the right track or helps to put the pieces together.

It hasn't failed me yet. Through my preparation and alignment with the method of divination, I have received profound insights. Moving through transitions or difficult situations can be a much more enjoyable experience when you have a glimpse of what is available to you from the other side.

In using any method of divination, it is your responsibility to filter the information received. You need to use discernment. The place in you that knows your highest truth will assist you. If you are told something that feels 'wrong', take a closer look. Are you in resistance, or is the messenger somehow off base? There is always a risk that the person providing the information will paint it with his or her own colors and brush strokes. Take what serves you and discard the rest. The process should be empowering. Even if you are told something that is difficult to hear, you will inherently know it is accurate and warrants attention.

Having a reading actually creates a broad experience that does not end when the physical reading is complete. You will find yourself reviewing the information and determining the ways you can apply it to your life. Then you will need to take action. Take a look at your goals and action plan. How can you incorporate your new learning into the plan you've been executing? Do some of your goals need to change in light of this new information or way of looking at things?

"The best things in life are free."

Beyond divination, there is much other ancient wisdom that offers value in our world today. The knowledge available in the universe is virtually unlimited. Here, however, only the ancient practices that people often use now will be described, coming to us from a broad spectrum of cultures, from Native Americans to the Chinese.

The Chinese often trace success or failure not so much to human actions, but to the workings of mysterious earth forces. Known as feng shui, literally 'wind' and 'water', these forces are believed to be responsible for determining health, prosperity, and good luck. Feng shui evolved from the observation that people are affected by their surroundings. If you change your surroundings, you change your life. The aim of feng shui is to harmonize the environment and energy flow to improve your life.

To the Chinese, feng shui is one component of a person's destiny. First is fate. You have no control over or say in this because it is determined by heaven. Luck follows and can be either man-made or from heaven. Next is feng shui, or earth luck Then comes charity and philanthropy, followed by education, experience, and self-development.

There are several forms of feng shui that are widely practiced. The most popular forms are the Compass School and the Black Hat Sect School. In the Compass School, the eight compass directions are emphasized, in the belief that they govern various aspects of your life. The Black Hat Sect School completely disregards compass directions, using instead the entrance of a room or structure as the main reference point. Colors, animal symbols, numbers, and elements are used to activate certain areas in the application of either school. With intent and consistent practice, any form of feng shui can produce positive results.

Crystals, another widely-used tool, have existed since the Earth was born. Their powers and properties have been recognized by cultures from all over the world, from the Greeks and Egyptians to the early Celtic and Native American civilizations.

Crystals also play a critical role in the legends surrounding Lemuria and Atlantis. It is said that, before the demise of these cultures, the wisdom gained through the use of crystals was committed into the care of the crystals themselves, for later access through the Akashic records by individuals ready to receive it.

The primary use of crystals relates to the unique vibrational forces inherent in specific stones and their attunement to similar forces within the human body. These powers are used to promote healing, general well-being, and spiritual growth. They are also believed to help people regain a state of balance with nature by raising their level of consciousness. Magickal powers are also attributed to crystals, so they are often carried or worn as talismans for protection, health, wealth, love, and good luck. This influence can be amplified by shaping the crystals in the form of a power symbol, whether it be related to the planets or to animals.

Animal spirits have been a source of wisdom and healing in many cultures, including the Cherokee, Lakota, Mayan, and Aztec tribes. They play an important role in shamanism and are often turned to for insight during self-development. These spirits, which represent the essence and qualities of different species, are a reminder to connect with the instinctual self.

By studying the characteristics of animals they are drawn to, individuals can gain awareness of their own subconscious beliefs and patterns. An animal spirit can be called on in dreams or meditations for guidance on how to manifest its specific strengths when needed in life. And an attraction to a certain animal at any given time is likely to be the universe's sign that there is something to be learned from its qualities.

Smudging is another practice drawn from native cultures worldwide. Native Americans, in particular, have used this cleansing ceremony throughout history. The belief is that certain sacred plants, like sage and cedar, agree to give their lives in return for respectful treatment so that humans may benefit from their smoke. Working with scents creates a connection with the instinctual self that can help change energies and trigger emotions, resulting in greater balance through purifying, cleansing, praying, and meditating. Smudging is most often used to dispel physical, mental, and emotional impurities and also to drive negative energy out of the home or office.

The increasing interest in ancient ways can be attributed to the search for 'something more' as people embrace the energy of the 'New Age', the Age of Aquarius that we are thought to be entering. Aquarius rules technology, individuality, and the intellect. As these characteristics take hold, people will not be labeled or placed under banners that overshadow their individuality. The self will become a greater focus. In this environment, individuals will continue seeking ways to put their past into more meaningful perspective, understand the present, and reveal alternatives for the future. Ancient wisdom is a significant step on this path.

Chapter 13

The Solution To Health Problems

"An ounce of prevention is worth a pound of cure."

The path to health is an integral part of your spiritual development. As you get to know yourself thoroughly, you come to know what supports your physical and spiritual health and what detracts from it.

Individuals who want a high level of health, as opposed to just an absence of debilitating illness, have learned in recent years to participate actively in their own care and not just defer passively to what the doctor says. Just like in any other area of your life, you have to take personal responsibility in the decision-making process in order to become empowered in creating your own state of perfect health.

This can be a very time-consuming process. You will need to seek several opinions. You will need to research the disease or illness and connect with your innate wisdom in developing your opinion about how the body should be brought back to its natural state of health.

Health is a gift that you just can't take for granted. Too often, you have to run yourself down to the point where you make your body a victim of infection in order to remember that. As you get to know yourself and your body better, you can sense when you're dangerously close to pushing yourself too far. At that point, you need to take the time to rebuild your strength. If you are exposed to a virus at a time when your body is strong, your immune system will take it on as a worthy opponent instead of easily giving in to the infection.

I recently survived a bout with strep throat, after being exposed to my niece and nephew who already had it. Of course, it wouldn't have mattered what I was exposed to. My body wasn't strong enough to fight anything off. And I knew the culprit — sleep deprivation. I had a little too much to do by day and a little too much fun by night. I might have been able to get away with it for a day or two, but day three produced a health-related meltdown.

This gave me the opportunity to focus on building up my reserve because it forced me to take the time. I needed to get through this battle and then focus on my health. For me, that means getting eight hours of sleep every night.

"Feed a cold, starve a fever."

The strep throat experience gave me a new appreciation for the body's ability to heal itself and for the steps along the way. I have learned to work with my body in the healing process, rather than trying to suppress the symptoms. Rather than taking something to put me out of the misery caused by having to constantly blow my nose, I blessed my body. I accepted that, the more I needed to blow my nose, the more I was ridding myself of the toxins that created my state of ill health in the first place. I watched as my body healed itself and, while it was not a comfortable thing to go through, it was inspiring.

When you experience the symptoms of a cold, your immune system kicks in to fight off the virus. Swelling and inflammation result, created primarily by the activation of the immune system and the resulting increase in blood flow. The body produces the inflammation in order to heal itself, because the greater blood circulation brings more white blood cells in to fight the viruses.

If the response is sufficient, whatever the disturbance is will be carried away by the natural flow of the body's blood supply. With a cold, the body also creates an abundance of mucus. This helps to flush out the membranes and discharge the waste products of the healing process.

If you choose to take a decongestant or antihistamine, you are directly combating the body's best efforts to heal. Over time, the immune system will become conditioned to the point that, eventually, it doesn't even try to generate the healing response. While you might have conquered the body in the short-term, you create dire consequences for the future.

This is also true of fevers. A fever is another way that the body cleanses itself naturally. For every degree Fahrenheit that the body temperature rises, the heart increases its rate by ten beats a minute and the body increases the urine filtration to better cleanse the system. At the same time, more blood forms to increase carbon dioxide and oxygen exchange. The heart sends this blood to the kidneys for filtration and elimination at a greater rate.

The higher metabolic rate in the system enables the body to do two things: it increases the rate of filtration and hastens the process of oxidation, two essential processes for ridding the body of toxins. When your temperature rises above 98.6 degrees, toxins, viruses and bacteria have less opportunity to survive in the body. In addition, in this elevated thermal state, your body produces larger quantities of interferon (a powerful anti-virus protein).

Ironically, whenever body temperature rises more than one or two degrees above 'normal', we are conditioned to consult a doctor or take a drug designed to lower it. Very few people allow their body temperature to rise naturally to 102 or 103 degrees Fahrenheit (or even higher), without interfering with the natural rhythm of the body's healing process.

When you interfere with the process, the result is that you often create more of what your body is trying to eliminate. For example, by suppressing the fever, you permit toxins to proliferate. You have unwittingly assisted in producing a powerful threat to your health because you have not resolved the underlying cause.

"Man cannot live on bread alone."

Many alternative forms of health care, that are low-tech and low cost, are often more appropriate than standard conventional medical treatment might be. The theory of homeopathy, for example, is fascinating. It basically operates on the principle that the more rapid the onset of the disease process, the more rapid the cure will be. The homeopath actually treats disease by introducing it into the body. The remedy triggers a healing response.

Conventional medicine places more value on techniques and technology than on the inherent healing power of nature we possess as human beings. It attempts to replace the body's natural healing response by quickly removing symptoms.

For example, instead of stimulating and strengthening the immune system to fight an ear infection in a toddler, a biomedical doctor will usually prescribe an antibiotic. The child often receives immediate relief, but at what price? The antibiotic wreaks havoc on the friendly bacteria needed for good digestion. Also, the child's immune system is not any stronger in terms of being able to ward off the next ear infection, which in essence creates a dependency on antibiotics. The price of immediate relief is the threat of future long-term health problems for the toddler.

When most of us go to a doctor, we are not in need of major technological miracles. Studies indicate that some 75 percent of visits to the family doctor are for stress or anxiety-related illnesses or for ailments, such as colds or flu, which will usually get better on their own.

Many of us go to the doctor, then, for education, emotional support, and a helping hand in mobilizing the body's own capacity to heal. We go to be heard and encouraged. And this is where we are most often disappointed, since even the most sensitive physician is severely limited by the constraints of a typical ten-minute office visit.

At the same time, if you go to a conventional doctor for an annual check-up, your health is assessed only from the results of your physical examination. Basically, the body is viewed as a biochemical machine in which the parts are separate and distinct. It is understood in ever-smaller units – that is, as tissues, organs, cells, molecules, and atoms. Science searches for the single underlying unit that makes up the body or, in the case of disease, a single pathogen or physical impairment that gives rise to symptoms. Little attention is given to diet, exercise, or personal psychological issues. Even less concern is given to the emotional, mental, spiritual, and social aspects of your life.

"The whole is greater than the sum of its parts."

In traditional medicine, health was instead defined to embrace virtually every aspect of human experience. This was based on the belief, held by the sages of East and West, that the body, mind, and spirit are a single, unified whole. All three of these human aspects are harmonized by an underlying entity that the ancients called the life force, a kind of spiritual energy that permeates the universe and manifests as individual beings.

In this view, the body is seen as part of ever-widening relationships. The workings of any single organ are looked at within the context of the whole. Thus, a health problem is approached as a symptom of an underlying imbalance in the body. Treatment consists of the healer working to strengthen the underlying life force that will enable the body's own healing mechanisms to overcome any illness or disorder.

When you are fully infused with this life force, the body and mind function optimally; that is, all of your cells, organs, and systems function at their full potential. In the same way that the whole is greater than the sum of its parts, you fully realize your potential. All your talents and abilities are available to you to express as you desire. Such a state, said the sages, brings with it an experience of unity with the ultimate reality, a harmony with the creator of life itself. This philosophy defined the methods used to maintain health and treat disease.

Edgar Cayce accessed this same wisdom in his work. When he died in 1945, he left documented records of readings he had given for more than six thousand different people over a 43-year period. Over 60 percent of his readings describe the physical disabilities of his subjects and suggest treatment for their ailments.

Cayce stated over and over again that everything you do and think is related to what you are as a complete human being. He said that the combination of what you think and eat together make what you are, physically and mentally. He taught that the physical body is the temple through which the mental, spiritual, and soul development must manifest.

Carl Jung expressed much the same viewpoint. He said that the purpose of life is to achieve a state of being that equips you to fully enjoy life and allows you to realize your full potential. Jung believed that, for those willing to follow the path of life with courage and intelligence, life leads inevitably to one's own inner nature, the true center of being. Jung called the path leading to self-knowledge the process of individuation. It's the process of becoming an individual, embracing one's own incomparable uniqueness.

It is the body that causes you to be here in the three-dimensional world. If it were not for your body, you wouldn't have to compete in the world of economics. You wouldn't need a house, food, clothes, or transportation. Therefore, the body must be kept in harmony and balance so that the parts that give us pleasure (the mind and spirit) can function to their greatest potential.

"No man is an island."

Both the good in our lives and the dis-ease result from mental thought patterns that form our experiences. Your thoughts and feelings influence your body via two kinds of mechanisms: the nervous system and the circulatory system. These are the pathways of communication between the brain and the rest of the body.

We all have many thought patterns that produce good, positive experiences, and these we enjoy. It is the negative thought patterns that produce uncomfortable, unrewarding experiences that really concern us. The goal is to change this dis-ease in your life into perfect health.

One way you can help heal yourself of habitual behavior, or old, constricting patterns that are lodged in your body or mind, is to work with your chakras. These seven, wheel-like energy centers spin at the inner core of your being. Each one is a focal point that corresponds to specific aspects of your physical, emotional, mental, and spiritual energies, each with its own characteristics and functions. Together, the seven chakras form the holistic network that coordinates your complicated mind/body system, thereby allowing your body, mind, and spirit to interact as one.

Whereas disease was once thought of as caused by genetics and germs (or essentially by lower chakra sources concerned with basic survival and self-preservation), the origin of disease is now viewed as stemming from toxic emotional stress levels (which relate to higher chakras). Diseases, symptoms, or distressing situations in your physical and emotional make-up are expressions of inhibited, misdirected, or conflicting rhythms in your body-mind. They create the need for you to look, whether consciously or otherwise, at all your energetic resources and pathways.

Rather than being seen as a form of punishment, disease or symptoms are essentially a wake-up call to indicate that something is not right. They tell you that you need to learn from what may have led to the disease, such as your thoughts, habits, or relationships. This will enable you to move on and redirect your life. In choosing a new direction, healing can occur.

There's an analogy between personal medicine and public well-being. The state of community exists first in consciousness as a way of being. The relationship you have with your body-mind is your primary community.

Just think about it. Your body is made up of cells. All of your body parts are made up of exactly the same 'stuff', yet it manifests as a nose, ears, and fingers. How does it know? Yet every distinct part serves a unique purpose, with unique roles and tasks. Each organ must do its part in the natural flow to convert what we consume into something that sustains life. When this community is working in harmony, you are supported in reaching your full potential.

A functional community creates joy, compassion, humility, love, and a sense of personal responsibility. As you bring this concept of community into the outside world, you can see how participating in a supportive community can be good for your health and the health of others. There has been much research suggesting that participation in an intentional community that promotes intimacy and the sharing of feelings is as important in the healing process as the techniques recommended by any healer.

Through intimacy comes love and, as psychotherapy and spiritual growth share the spotlight more and more, love becomes recognized as a force that influences biological activity. Most life crises have love at their core. These crises often are the cause of illness. Healing begins with the repair of emotional injuries.

In order to heal physically, you have to heal the emotional issues that caused the illness in the first place. Our entire medical model is being reshaped around the power of the heart. In other words, love helps us heal ourselves.

Healing is possible through acts of forgiveness. Jesus taught that forgiveness is a spiritual act of perfection. It is also physically healing. It isn't an option; it is a necessity. When you forgive someone who you perceive has hurt you, it is an act of loving yourself. This creates the environment needed for healing in your body.

"Don't make a mountain out of a mole hill."

All emotions are grounded in various parts of the body. A person with a healthy liver and gall bladder will have a balanced temperament, but one whose liver and gall bladder are troubled will likely suffer outbursts of anger and ill-temper. This leads to rash decisions. When the liver and gall bladder are balanced and healthy, decisions are made from emotional equilibrium. Since these organs are primarily responsible for ridding the body of toxins it is easy to see how a toxic lifestyle eventually takes its toll.

Maintaining your health is critical to problem-solving. Rather than being the result of searching and seeking, connecting with your spiritual source or highest truth occurs by removing the blocks that prevent your knowing. Like opening the blinds in a dark room, you open to the new and unexpected by opening to your spiritual nature.

Buddha taught that suffering was due to a lack of knowledge. It isn't shameful to suffer. It exists so that you may learn to be free of ignorance and recognize your true nature as a spiritual being. As you move through the suffering, you arrive at an important point on the healing journey. You are ready to separate yourself from the suffering and reject the cause.

Take, for example, the stress response. The stress response describes the changes that occur in the body when you experience what you perceive to be a challenging or threatening situation. It is all about perception. The body's response is the same whether the threat is real or imagined.

The magnitude of the changes is directly related to how serious you think the situation is and how you feel about your ability to handle the threat effectively. The more confident you are in your ability to handle the challenge, the less stress there is involved. As you build your problem-solving skills and, correspondingly, your confidence that the universe is supporting you through your life experiences, you will find that stress is a thing of the past.

If you have done your work, you have a sense of self that is strong enough to realize that you have dishonored your inner essence (the God within, your higher self) by finding comfort in the discomfort of anxiety and fear. You turn your back on suffering and move in a new direction. This may create temporary chaos in your life, but somehow you know you need it to move through your comfort zone.

"Prevention is the best medicine."

The human body is a truly amazing thing. It runs with such precision, despite the abuse it is constantly under. Most people don't treat it with nearly as much care as they do other 'complex machines' they deal with.

Compare it with how we treat our cars, for example. We wouldn't think of putting substandard gasoline in the tank of our cars but regularly eat foods that we know don't support optimal health. No matter how long the list of things to do before going, it's common procedure to prioritize getting an oil change and routine check-up before taking a road trip. In contrast, we don't do the preventive maintenance necessary to keep our bodies physically fit.

According to biologists, the life span of a species is from eight to ten times the age at which it is first capable of reproduction. Theoretically, then, man should live to at least 120 to 150 years of age. So we don't really die of old age. To die of old age would mean that all the vital organs would be worn out proportionately. In reality, we die because one or more of our vital organs breaks down. One vital part wears out too early in relation to the rest of the body. This is what happens when preventive maintenance is ignored.

Edgar Cayce's views on man's youth and potential longevity were consistent with these natural laws found in the animal kingdom. It's no surprise, then, that he consistently prescribed exercise in his readings. He recommended making the body physically, as well as mentally, tired and suggested that the poisons in the system from non-elimination would disappear as a result.

I have encouraged you many times throughout this book to take a walk whenever you are having difficulty finding a solution to a problem you are facing. Exercise is one of the most powerful preventive medicines available to you and the surest way to an attitude adjustment. It is an important therapeutic tool in repairing the ravages of disease and also clears your energy field on every level. Overall, exercise is essential to the maintenance of health, mental equilibrium, and spiritual harmony.

The other critical element of preventive maintenance has to do with what you eat and drink. Because the blood's state of health is dependent on what you consume, your diet is critical to healthy living.

The blood that goes through your intestines is the same blood that goes through your brain. It feeds your muscles, which support your bones, which allow you to maintain your physical structure.

Any condition present in the body can be traced in the blood supply. The blood stream carries the rebuilding forces to the body. It also takes the used forces and eliminates them through their proper channels and systems.

"You are what you eat."

As I have taken a front seat in the process of creating a state of perfect health in my life, I have seen first-hand how critically important every decision is when I am choosing what I will consume. I had always eaten pretty healthy, no 'junk food' or 'fast food'. I ate fish and rarely used fattening sauces or spreads. I had learned that my body was intolerant of caffeine and gave that up after suffering from severe headaches.

I drank wine occasionally and would give in to the temptation when a chocolate chip cookie was put in front of me. But, all in all, anyone would have pronounced my diet 'healthy'.

While my diet was pretty healthy, I ate good food but not much of it was 'live'. And I ate a lot of pasta. Since I have a sensitivity to wheat, I was in essence poisoning myself every time I ate a big Italian meal, in large part because my system was already stressed. The real problem was my approach to life. I was bombarded with stressful situations constantly and, over time, had less and less energy left in my body's detoxification process to deal with any added stresses from other sources.

After many years of leading this far too stressful life, I sought the advice of a medical doctor turned homeopath that came highly recommended by several of my friends. He spent several hours evaluating my approach to life and what was and was not contributing to my state of ill health at the time.

Among several things, he insisted that I begin juicing fresh vegetables on a regular basis. My dad had been doing this for years, and I told him that I likened it to drinking dirt. At this point though, I was desperate enough to feel better that I told the doctor I'd give it a try. It was the most profound experience I've ever had related to healing.

As I began consuming live enzymes, my body rid itself of toxins that had been building up within it for 35 years. I was 15 pounds heavier than I would have liked to be and lost it in a matter of six weeks. I didn't really alter my diet much, just less sugar and no pasta. It was amazing.

After I began juicing, I realized how much live food it really takes to support a healthy system. I'm surprised I survived as long as I did. If I am having a stressful day, I can drink a glass of fresh vegetable juice and feel the 'cloud' lifting virtually immediately.

Let me define fresh. We're not talking about V-8. Fresh means it was run through the juicer in the last 30 minutes. The closer it is to being picked and juiced, the fresher it is (and the more beneficial). You can't buy carrot juice that was juiced yesterday and accomplish the same thing.

What you are after here is the phytochemicals. They begin dissipating as soon as the juice is extracted. You're better off drinking a not so fresh juice if the alternative is a soda, but if you're after the effects of juicing, the law of diminishing return is put into motion as soon as the fruit or vegetable is picked.

After several months of working with this homeopathic doctor, I went back to his office for a check-up. I had started having occasional headaches and wasn't sure what was causing them. When I described my condition, he asked me what I had been eating. It only took me a few minutes to figure it out.

I was feeling so good that I thought I could cheat a little. There was a frozen yogurt place that I had been frequenting. He said I could probably get away with it once a week. For me, it was easier to just steer clear.

It isn't easy to live life demonstrating that you understand that you are what you eat. There is a price to pay. My body is very sensitive now. I don't get away with much. I love Italian food, but I have learned to eat risotto as an alternative to pasta. A big pasta meal gives me an immediate headache. One glass of wine is fine, but two keeps me awake half the night. But the payoff is worth the effort, a lesson I learned the hard way.

I hope this will help you keep in mind, too, the importance of taking good care of yourself and treasuring your health. The state of your physical health is directly related to your quality of life, therefore health is a reflection of how you choose to live. Are you prioritizing your health in a way that sends a clear message to the universe that you understand this? It is the most important thing you have to take with you on this journey.

Chapter 14

When Your Supply Is Lacking

"Money makes the world go round."

While some people might be jealous of the celebrity that makes millions of dollars for one feature film, I love hearing the life stories of people who dared to dream big and realized their aspirations. I choose to be grateful that the person has shown me what is possible. These are 'regular' people, like us, who have been willing to do what it takes to pursue their dreams. While it seems like they have the world by the tail, many of them will tell you that they have suffered a great deal in their lifetime. Money hasn't been able to solve every problem.

While money doesn't buy happiness, it does make life easier. For me, beyond putting food on the table and a roof over my head, it buys experiences. I have been able to travel, pursue growth opportunities, and take the time off to do it because I have embraced money and the power it wields.

Many of us have been conditioned to hold limited beliefs about money for fear it would take over our lives. "If I love money too much, I will turn control of my life over to the equivalent of the devil and get lost in the murky swamp." So how do you maintain a healthy attitude towards money, without limiting the universe's divinely planned supply for you?

It starts with accepting that money is what makes the world go around. You might argue this, but love, for example, would be happy sitting perfectly still. Money demands to be put into circulation. It is most beneficial when used in a way that you personally perceive as a life enhancement. To make money a source of light in your life, you need to use its energy wisely. You don't want to waste it as if it had no value; instead, put it to good use.

Good use is a very personal thing. Everyone has his or her own unique approach to spending money. One person's bargain is another's splurge. For example, I have a friend that does his own car repairs because he is uncomfortable with what the garage would charge him in labor. In contrast, he will spend freely on a great bottle of wine. Another friend spends money every week getting her nails done but won't hire a housekeeper to help her keep her home in order. How many times do you see people begging for money on the street with a cigarette in their mouth? A strange prioritization, if you ask me, but then no one asked me. I have my own money spending quirks, so, to each his own.

Your money is just that, your own. You have to decide what feels like an appropriate use of it for yourself. Once you've begun the process, you will probably need to evaluate how much is enough for you personally. Spend some time understanding what your version of 'enough' is. This is critical in the process of creating abundance in your life. If abundance is lacking, it is certainly related in some way to your subconscious beliefs about what you deserve and what you should be satisfied with.

You might ask, "If the universe is so abundant, why do people go hungry? Why are people homeless?" They have yet to claim their own personal 'enough'. Homeless people, in some way, have chosen to be homeless. Their beliefs and actions have created the situation they're in. And there is plenty of food on the planet to feed everyone; it just isn't distributed evenly. As more and more people open themselves to the concept that we are all one, the uneven distribution will no longer be allowed to continue.

While we can see that it is only right to step in and help those in need, they have to do their part too. When you give money to homeless people on the street, for example, you are actually supporting them in that lifestyle. The people and businesses affected by the presence of homeless people would be the first to tell you, "Don't give them money." Instead, give to the shelters, provide clothing and food, offer them work. They need an opportunity and the means to use it.

"Where your mind wanders, your life follows."

As you begin working with the techniques in this book, you will find that you begin manifesting more than you ever thought possible. If you haven't prepared yourself for this, your subconscious will find a way to sabotage you. Rather than working to become comfortable in the new life you are creating, the subconscious wants to go back to living within the old program.

Pretending that your subconscious doesn't have that kind of power and control just doesn't work. You have to live where it lives, in meditation or in whatever ways you can get there. Once you understand how it is undermining your efforts, it is fairly easy to begin to turn things around.

A subtle shift can have immediate impact. Get your subconscious to begin working in cooperation with you, and the battle is won. All you need to do is define what you consider 'enough', abundant enough, and get out of your own way. Once you do that, you will certainly keep growing it, as the universe begins to support you in creating what you say you need to be financially comfortable.

My mother is really good at manifesting money. She may not do it on a large scale, but whenever she is feeling a bit stretched, somehow the universe comes through for her in brilliant displays of unexpected perfection.

As this starts to work for you, the results will be surprising. You will be tempted to say 'unbelievable'. I caution you to be careful in your choice of words. If the manifestation is unbelievable, it won't likely reoccur. Isn't it actually "believable, amazing, incredible, and expected?" You put the effort forth to make it happen. Didn't you expect that the universe would support you?

Your attitude towards money creates a mindset. This mindset produces thoughts that go out into the universe and put the wheels in motion. So all you need to do is control your thoughts. All you need to do is control your thoughts. It is amazing how easy that is to write even though I know how challenging it is to put into action.

There is a little book that I can wholeheartedly recommend as required life reading. It's The Game of Life and How to Play It by Florence Scovel Shinn. This book was recommended to me several years ago and has had a profound impact on my life. In a few hours, you see life in a whole new light.

Ms. Shinn wrote this book in 1925. At the time, she said we were just beginning to wake up to the power and abundance of the universe that is available to us. While I can see that we've made progress, it's amazing to me that, 75 years later, we are still struggling with these concepts. It just shows you how tough they are to consistently put into practice.

We constantly give the universe casual requests that we don't back up with much action. To really have an impact, you can use a symbol or charm, a ritual, or any other similar process to say to the universe, *"I know I have asked you for lots of help, but this is where we really need to focus – right now!"*

We talked about feng shui in an earlier chapter. You'll recall that feng shui is a practice used to create a balanced environment that attracts positive energy and cures specific concerns. It has gained widespread use over the last several years for many reasons, namely its application in manifesting wealth and abundance through the part of your space known as your wealth corner. When you activate this area, you send a message to the universe that you are prepared to receive what is rightfully yours.

There are many ways to activate your wealth corner. I like to use a money frog. The money frog represents good fortune and money-making and, depending on its placement, can help you attract extraordinary wealth, as well as career and mentor luck.

At one point, I was speaking to the owner of a feng shui supply store about the different sizes and finishes of the frogs the store carried. I was particularly attracted to the giant money frog. It is 20 times the average size and looks quite regal. When I asked what I could expect from such a large version of this symbol, I was told that the larger the problem I was trying to solve, the bolder my statement needed to be.

That was all I needed to hear. I brought it home and put it in the appropriate area, used the activation technique, and let it go to work. A few days later, I received a very large check that was totally unexpected.

Another idea, recommended by the author Catherine Ponder, is to keep play money in your wallet. Every time you go there, you'll see your wallet stuffed with cash. Soon, the play money will be replaced with the real stuff.

When you use symbols like this, it isn't so much the symbol itself that manifests what you desire or require. It is your intention. The symbol simply serves to remind you. It helps you focus your energy and lets the universe know you're serious.

Why would you need symbols to help you focus? Think about it. Most money never even touches your hands. It moves electronically. It is the belief of money. When you write a check, it is a perceived reduction in supply. When you deposit a check, you have the belief that your supply has increased (and fortunately the bank backs you up). I prefer to view this as a sign from the universe that my supply is abundant and limitless. If I have manifested some money, then I can certainly keep doing it, right?

As you begin to manifest abundance in your life, you will want to share your miracles with those close to you. This can be very dangerous, if the people you're sharing with don't practice the same techniques. Unless you are consistently encouraging and supporting one another, there is a good chance that you will get the wind knocked out of your sails. If you do unwittingly share with someone and they try to bring you down, say, "Thanks for sharing," and move on as quickly as possible. There is no room for non-believers in the process.

Manifesting requires you to be fully present with the process. The most difficult part of this process is staying focused, intentional, and in a state of heightened expectation. You need to align yourself with people that help you do that or stick to your own company.

"Stagnation breeds disease."

The Bible tells us our barns should be full. We've all seen people who are so busy keeping their barns full that they don't enjoy their money. They are wealthy by most people's standards, but they live as if they are steeped in poverty.

For these people, money is an unhealthy influence in their lives. They are more concerned with the piece of paper that tells them how much is in their bank account than with the experiences that the money has been provided to them for. These people will eventually create stagnation in their supply. Stagnation breeds disease and is characterized by a lack of flow.

A friend of mine knows two older gentlemen that are roommates. I met these characters on several occasions, and they are delightful in most ways, until it comes to spending money. I don't think they'd even qualify as poster children for 'frugal'. Their approach to life is very limited. One of these men had several hundred thousand dollars that he had invested. The more he held on to his money, the more was taken away. The last I knew he was battling in court for the majority of it.

When you attempt to hoard and save, it has the opposite effect. The universe will send you situations that force you to deal with your attitude towards money and how you use it to enhance your life. If you trust the universe as an abundant servant that wants nothing more than for you to live a limitless life, why would you deny yourself anything?

I'm not saying you should go out and throw your money away on things that don't mean anything to you. That dishonors your self, the money, and the universe. When you release your money freely on things that are important to you, you create space for the universe to manifest more. The more you circulate, the more you manifest.

There has been much written about tithing, and it makes sense to me that I would systematically put back into circulation a part of what has been provided by the universe. But when I decided that I wanted to start working with this principle, I really had to do some soul-searching. While it seems to resonate with my understanding of how the universe works, I had a problem with the whole religious aspect.

The books I read clearly indicated that a tithe would not be recognized unless it was given to a spiritual organization, specifically an organization that had been instrumental in my own development. For me, there was no such animal. I grew up in the Christian church and, while I don't have any horror stories about the spiritual education I received, something was always lacking. My spiritual foundation was built on my own studies and discoveries.

I felt that nature was the 'organization' that had supported me most in my spiritual development. If I gave to organizations that benefited the environment, would God not recognize my gifts? If I chose to believe this, I would create a judgmental God for myself. This is what turned me away from organized religion in the first place. God doesn't judge. God recognizes my good intentions and supports me in whatever I choose to do.

And then there was the suggestion that you tithe ten percent of your income. That gets a little hazy — ten percent of gross, net, or whatever you receive?

Anyway, I pursued it because I really felt it was the right thing to do, no matter how I did it. I always write my tithe checks at the end of the month. These checks are but a symbol of the rich substance of the universe that is available to me. When I send them, I give thanks that 100 times this amount (or ten times ten) is now on its way to me. I also give thanks that it appears quickly so that every financial obligation is immediately and completely met, with plenty to share and spare, under grace in God's own wise and wonderful ways.

One month I was feeling a little squeezed financially and, as a result, was also feeling a bit tight-fisted. Yet, I said a little prayer and let my tithe checks go out anyway. The last week of the month, just as things were closing in, I received a small miracle.

I had a truck for sale for several months and someone came, literally out of nowhere, and bought it. The events surrounding this were nothing less than miraculous. It wasn't really what I needed, but it *was* a sign of land, and a pretty significant one at that.

A week later, I was seeking guidance in meditation and received intuitionally that I needed to work on this chapter. I had originally planned to write this chapter last because I was a little arrogant in my belief that I had this stuff 'figured out'. I could save this for last because it would be easy.

Any time my ego gets a bit out of control, I am confronted with just what I need to keep it in check. That explains being financially strapped; I realized that I had created this situation through my own inattention to several details in my financial life. I needed to do first things first and take care of the loose ends.

It also explains getting the guidance to write this chapter immediately, instead of last. I still have lots to learn about manifesting financial abundance, and the time had come to put my effort where my mouth was. All I needed to do was walk my talk. I was reminded that this is all part of the process. I need to enjoy the journey even when the road is a little bumpy. The universe has never let me down. Why would it start now? I just needed to make some minor adjustments to get things flowing again.

"A first impression is a lasting impression."

My career is that of a service provider. I have to own my value and project that into the universe, in order to be rewarded as I perceive appropriate. When I am in the market for services myself, I keep the mirror close by. If I am questioning the value of services being provided to me, I slow down and evaluate the impact this has on the perceived value I have for my own services.

Sometimes I am indeed just being overcharged. In times like these, I am comfortable with delaying the service until I can find a more cost-effective alternative. Other times, I am just not in reality. The services I need are worth what the provider is asking; I just need to adjust my perception. It helps to remind myself that I want my services to be perceived as highly valuable and this instance might be an opportunity to see where I am still holding myself back. When I can give someone else what I want to receive, I am putting into action a very powerful universal law.

Still, I've never fully understood the concept of barter. Actually, that's not true. I just haven't seen it work really well. Someone always feels like they got the short end of the stick. If I agree to provide you with services and you agree to provide me with goods, then shouldn't it be, by virtue of the fact that we agreed to the terms, a fair exchange? When you come to my office and I tell you I will charge you $100 to do something for you, you have a choice to accept the price or go elsewhere. Theoretically, the barter system should work the same way, but somehow we trust money more than perceived value.

Money defines the value of something. It works because we all basically live by the same rules. The problem doesn't seem to be one of how much money is worth but more one of our own self-worth. How much money do you deserve?

The universe will provide you with perfect pay for perfect service. The key here is perfect service. If you are not fully engaged in your work, you will be rewarded in line with that. When work feels empty, you will feel empty. This attracts emptiness, eventually in your pocketbook.

Likewise, it has been said that you never get a second chance to make a first impression, and I concur. If you don't present an image consistent with what someone would expect of a successful person in your position, then you will have a much higher hurdle to jump to gain that person's respect and trust for what you have been engaged to do for them.

In a recent article of Business Week (March 19, 2001), it was reported that some companies (in light of the dot-com failures and the waning urge to impress a younger crowd) are rethinking the dress code and reverting to more professional attire. They say business casual has detracted from the professionalism of the workplace.

For years, I wore a suit to the office every day. As a CPA, it was important to reflect a professional, confident image. When I interviewed applicants for positions at the firm, I would talk to them about professional dress. It is important to understand that you are attempting to capture someone else's image of what success looks like. If you are a repair person, that might be a pressed and clean uniform. In a clothing store, the clerk should be dressed to encourage the customers to spruce up their wardrobe by making a fashion statement. In my business, it was a suit.

You could resist this. "If someone is going to draw an opinion about me and my capabilities from what I'm wearing, then that's their problem." I can assure you that they are and that you are guilty of the same thing. You can make things much harder for yourself and complain that you seem to always be sitting on the bench, or you can choose to play the game 'well' and dress for success. Try this and see how the universe responds through all the people you come into contact with.

Work doesn't have to be 'hard', although it might be. Even if you really enjoy what you're doing, you might feel stretched and a little stressed about it. But when your heart is in it, perfect service is an easy thing. Work is your playground, the place where you get to practice what you've learned and develop new skills and techniques. Even those jobs that some people might consider tedious or monotonous can be creatively inspirational, if approached with the proper mindset. Remember, it's all about the process.

I have been closing in on a project I've been working on for several months now. It is something I've been talking about doing for several years and finally made the time to do. In the process, I have learned so much about myself, my path, and how the universe works. More importantly, I know that I have only begun this journey.

Having a somewhat critical nature (it's that stellium in Virgo in the first house that I mentioned earlier), I had been a little hard on myself for taking so long to bring this project to the front burner. If only I had started it when I began talking about it several years ago, think how far along I'd be. I have realized (or been reminded) that it doesn't work that way.

I needed the experiences over the past several years to fully prepare myself. If I would have tried to force things sooner, the experience would have been painful and what I might have produced wouldn't have been nearly as rich. While it is my responsibility to put things in motion, I must wait for the universe to open the channels to manifest what I am putting energy into. All in divine time, and divine time is beyond my control. In the meantime, my job is to enjoy life and the journey, using every obstacle as an opportunity.

Chapter 15

Resolving Relationship Problems

"Be careful what you wish for."

You can only grow so much, on your own, without sharing your life with other human beings. There is a lot of work to do individually, but when you really want to test how far you've come and what you've actually mastered, a relationship provides the perfect stage.

There is something undeniably raw about putting yourself in a position of vulnerability with another person. When you are exposed in this way, it's like your buttons are sitting right there in plain view. Whomever you've chosen to be there with has tremendous power. They can choose to push the buttons and see what happens, or they can recognize that you have given them this power and honor both of you by working with you as you grow to understand what the buttons do.

A relationship reveals your best and worst self. At its best, you can see all that you can be (and already are). At its worst, you see every flaw and how much work you still have to do. Even this can be an incredible gift. When the student is ready, the teacher appears.

After a two year 'dry spell', I started dating a man I met at a local health food store. The person didn't appear to fit into my life. We were very different. Still there was something that needed to be explored.

One day I stumbled across a list I had made of the characteristics I'd like to have in a partner. It was amazing! This man was an answer to 90 percent of that list. I'm sure you've heard the phrase, "Be careful what you ask for." If I have ever understood what that meant, this was the time.

As the relationship developed, it was obvious that we were not even close to right for each other. We brought out the worst in each other. I was the worst version of myself, and it was humiliating. After we would reach an impasse on something we were dealing with, I would reflect on my behavior and think, "Who was that person sitting in my body?" We were both reluctant to give up and prolonged the agony way longer than was useful.

While there were many lessons learned, the freight train of awareness came in realizing that I needed to burn that list. I obviously had no idea what I needed and what would really work for me. This man fit the list, but he came in a distorted package. I realized I need to ask for the perfect man for me and trust that the universe knows perfection on a much more profound level than I may ever get to.

So, what do you do when you finally recognize the pattern you are repeating? They show up in so many different ways that it takes a discerning eye to recognize them. In my case, I now know I attract unavailable men. Whew!! I said it. I must admit, it isn't easy to put this out there for the world to see. Now that I do see the pattern, I have full personal responsibility for deciding what I want to do with it.

This kind of stuff doesn't consciously happen. It is coming from a very deep place that works on your energy field. There is an unmet need, a hole if you will, that is projecting itself into the world. When you understand that no void goes unfilled, it makes perfect sense that you attract something to take up that space. You attract relationships that fill a void until you fill the void yourself and can attract what you really need.

Now is a really good time to start asking questions. The only person with the answers is you. If you keep looking, you will find the hole, and that is only the beginning. Once you recognize there is a hole, you have to figure out how to fill it in constructive ways, with conscious choice. How can you love yourself, in the ways that your subconscious is expecting someone else to do for you? You can't attract what you say you want until you are that yourself. That means you are a whole person – or to put it another way 'holeless'.

At that point, you can make the quantum shift from, "What can you do for me?" to *"What can we create together?"* In a relationship, you should be the best version of yourself, the greatest 'you' you can imagine. You need to want that for your partner too. Can you honestly say, *"I want for you what you want for you"* and mean it, no matter what the personal consequences?

"Look out for number one."

So, how do you become your best self? You have to create your own happiness and pursue your own dreams. The 'you' that emerges will be someone who will create a meaningful relationship with whomever you choose.

What have you been waiting to do until you have someone to do it with? Don't wait a moment longer. Start out with something simple – as non-threatening as possible. Would you like to go to the museum or theater? Take a hike to a special place? It's wonderful to share experiences with someone you really care about that feels the same way about you, but there is real juice in experiencing things by yourself too.

I was a partner in an accounting firm for many years. We regularly supported the philanthropic community and attended many special events. It's fun to get dressed up and have a great night out, especially when it benefits a good cause. When I was married, these events were really special. I always had a 'date'. When my partner and his wife were there, it was like a double date, with the added pleasure of having all our friends around.

After I got divorced, things changed 'a bit' (the understatement of the millennium). These events turned into painful experiences. I tried lots of alternatives. Not going wasn't good for me, the business, or the community. I could invite a male friend, but that was usually not reliable because a girlfriend expected to be the date. I decided to go alone to several of these events. While it was great to be at the party, it just wasn't the same.

Once I felt that I had overcome my fear of going alone and could make a choice that was right for me (not fear-based), I chose to do what made me happy. It was preferable to not attend. I had to go through the process to get through the fear. It was rewarding on so many levels.

I realized that I have spent many a lonely hour in the company of several hundred people. Lonely is something you feel when you aren't in the company of people that you resonate with. Without a meaningful connection, a warm body does nothing to fill the loneliness hole.

There are different ways of dealing with loneliness. Some people pull away from the crowd and resign themselves to spend time alone. They may not really be spending time alone though; the television can be a comforting and intoxicating friend, for example.

I was married to a person that would come home every day after work and sit for hours watching television. My clearest recollection is of trying to strike up a conversation and having him tell me (after I had asked a question several times) that he was watching television and shouldn't be interrupted. How many times can someone watch the same story on CNN and feel like it is critical to his daily activities?

The truth is that the television was a very good friend to him. It didn't challenge him or expect anything from him. It was easy spending time with the TV. We were both lonely and making friends with whatever gave us comfort. Other people choose to 'make busy' when they are faced with feeling lonely. They cram their lives full of activities so that, by the time the week is over, they have had no time to feel the void. The only way to really cure loneliness is to realize that it is part of the illusion. You are never really alone, and all it takes is a few minutes in meditation to experience that.

Now, I don't hesitate to go to a movie or out to dinner by myself, if that's what feels right in the moment. I do what makes me happy, and the 'me' this creates is a much better partner for it.

An important part of the process is bringing what you've learned into the light so you can examine it. *Being* with someone else doesn't make you whole. But *sharing* with someone else can help you experience all of yourself and define who you are so you feel more whole.

"You're either a leader or a follower."

Sometimes, after a long day of decision-making, it's nice to have someone else decide what movie to see or where to go to dinner; it's easier just to follow. But when you're talking about your own life, you need to be the leader. In order to create your destiny, you have to know where you want to go and take off in that direction. If you're following someone else, you're creating their destiny rather than your own.

I have always been an independent, "I can take care of myself (and everyone else)" person. When I moved to Colorado, I was faced with building a new infrastructure for my life. After 29 years in Las Vegas, I knew just where to go whenever I needed anything. There was always someone with just the right skill set to help me with whatever my current issue happened to be.

After several days of traveling, I showed up in Colorado, ready to begin my new life. Little did I know how new it was really going to be! I had lined up a couple of men to help my friend and I move things from storage to my new space. A couple of hours before we were supposed to meet them with the truck, the phone rang and I found out they wouldn't be available to help us. My friend convinced me that we could handle it ourselves, and I was anxious to get settled, so we decided to jump in with both feet.

It was one of those times when I didn't slow down long enough to really think things through. The truck we rented wasn't what I had requested, and there wasn't a hand-truck available. We were supposed to have the truck back that evening, and it was already 2:00 in the afternoon. Fortunately, my friend was pretty much 'super-human' and handled the heavy stuff, but I still needed to balance things and pick up the other end.

By 8:30, it was getting dark. We were feeling the pressure to finish what we could, because the storage closed at 9:00 (not to mention that we were exhausted). One last piece… a big desk that was extremely heavy and awkwardly shaped. We got it just to the top of the truck ramp when he slipped. Then I slipped, the desk went flying, and I did the first cartwheel of my adult life. I can assure you it was nowhere near a perfect ten. My entire body weight landed on my extended right arm, from about five feet in the air. I heard a bone crack and knew I was in trouble. The security guard charged with locking up the facility showed up and I found myself laying on the asphalt with two men staring at me, asking me if I was okay. I knew I wasn't okay, but I just wanted to lay there and reverse the clock a few minutes. The damage was done.

The next thing I knew, I was on my way to the hospital. For the first time in my life, I would be the patient. The diagnosis? A broken and dislocated right elbow. And, yes, I *am* right-handed. Ouch! So now the move that was totally under control had careened over the ledge, and fortunately I had landed in a ditch. It still required me to dig out.

The first thing I had to do was adjust my attitude. It wasn't going to do me any good to stress about what I wasn't able to do and how much this would set me back. I did have the choice to use this opportunity to learn something about myself.

After acknowledging that, I had to confront being dependent. For the first couple of days, I really couldn't do anything, and I was limited in what I could do for a couple of months. I had to accept help from wherever it came. More importantly, I had to *ask* for help, not a comfortable thing. Yet, help was there for me.

I set realistic expectations and took it one day at a time. The settling-in process would have taken me about two weeks with all my faculties. Instead, it took me two months. What I learned in the process I might not otherwise have realized in two years. The key is to recognize that you must live interdependently.

There is a middle-ground between independence and dependence — collaboration. Some people might call it compromise, but it feels a little bit different to me. When you collaborate, you recognize that you both (or all) have a problem. You are confident that there is a solution that works for everyone and that, by putting your heads together, the most amazingly perfect resolution will rise to the surface and provide you with not only relief but inspiration.

There is nothing quite like working through a problem with someone and coming up with a solution that really feels good. Of course, you have to be willing to let go of how you think you want things to be resolved. You have to trust that there is a solution that is perfect for everyone. There is no right or wrong; everyone's input is valuable and leads to the outcome.

Going into the zone of 'not knowing' can really push your security buttons. "I know I want things to change but only in a way that is comfortable for me." That isn't win/win. Win/win looks different: *"I know things need to change, and I trust that I will be supported through the process."* The most important result is that everyone is blessed by whatever is decided.

There is value in being independent, and there is certainly a time where you need to be dependent, but the juice is in the interdependency. *"How do I really share my life with other people so that we are all blessed by the relationship?"*

"Do unto others as you would have them do unto you."

If you're like most people, you'd rather stick your toe in the water and wade in only until you're comfortable. When you get to the point where you feel like you could get pulled under, you turn back and retreat to a place where you feel like you are in control.

It's when you *do* get pulled under that you are forced to let go of what you thought you wanted and trust that there is something available to you that is beyond your imagination. You can't sit on the fence. You're either in it, or you're not. Don't fool yourself.

What would your partner say about the depth of your commitment? Are you really in it together? You aren't truly vulnerable unless you're willing to get hurt. If you look at your relationships, can you honestly say that you gave yourself freely and that you turned over every stone?

Are your relationships based on unconditional acceptance? This gets a little cloudy. Even if you choose not to *love* someone, based on who they are, you can *accept* them unconditionally. In fact, that is the only choice to make – for yourself and for them. If *I* want for you what *you* want for you, then wouldn't I accept you both as you are and as you are becoming? Without that, there can be no meaningful relationship.

If you know that I am sitting on the fence, trying to decide whether I will accept you just the way you are, how willing will you be to enter that space of vulnerability that ultimately fosters intimacy? To find a good friend or partner, you need to be a good friend and partner. Are you giving to others what you want to receive?

Most of us would agree that a good friend is someone you can really trust with your deepest secrets. Someone who knows you and loves you just the way you are. Spending time with a close friend can be a way to charge your batteries.

With like-minded uplifting people, you feel comforted just being in their presence or talking to them. A true friend won't always tell you what you want to hear; sometimes they'll tell you what you *need* to hear. The appropriate messenger shows up at the perfect time. When that messenger is also a good friend, are you willing to drop your defenses and listen without judgment?

"Honesty is the best policy."

To achieve good relationships with others requires intimacy. You can't really create intimacy, only the environment that fosters it, and intimacy is fostered in an environment of honesty and truth. If you don't have a close relationship with yourself, you may have difficulty getting to your highest truth. Your highest truth is the 'whole truth and nothing but the truth' as you know it today. You might make a discovery tomorrow that changes your highest truth, but what's important is that what you share today is genuinely honest, based on the 'you' that you are today.

I love it when someone says, "Can I be really honest with you?" If you're like me and respond, "Yes, please be completely honest," then you better take a deep breath and prepare yourself to listen, without jumping forward to rebuttal. It doesn't do you any good to candy-coat things or have things candy-coated for you. You are going to have to deal with it at some point. There's no time like the present.

I was talking to a friend one night, relating my experiences of the prior year. While it's behind me now and I've sort of numbed myself to it, I was the proverbial pinball in the pinball machine as I experienced it. Everything happened so fast that I didn't really have time to catch my breath before I was bounced right back into the game. Between events, there was that period of anticipation, like when the pinball is falling to the bottom of the machine. What was going to happen next? Would I go right through the middle and be out of play, or would the flipper catch me and send me back through the amusement park? The universe kept putting me back into play. I had lots of adjustments to make and not a whole lot of time to make them.

Anyway, when I was done relating the year's events to my friend, he said, "Can I be honest with you?" Deep breath. Of course I wanted him to be really honest... and he was. He told me that he heard what I was saying but couldn't feel it. It was all just stuff that happened. You really had to live through the conversation to realize how profound that was, but the light bulb flashed.

The past year had unfolded so quickly that I hadn't taken the time and space to really process it. I woke up the next morning right in the middle of it. It all came back to me in living color. There was so much learning that still needed to take place. Why go through all that and not really 'get it'? I would just have to re-experience it at some point.

If my friend hadn't been willing to be honest with me, I might never have found the treasure that was available to me. Of course, I had to be willing to hear what he was saying and let it in.

Tough love can be the most caring love there is. It is just as tough on the person giving it as it is on the one receiving it. When you know that the most loving thing to do for someone is to tell them what they need to hear (not necessarily what they want to hear), ask for guidance and the universe will help you find the right words at the right time. The person you must first be true to is yourself.

Another aspect to this is realizing when it is time to rethink a relationship in your life. When you have people you care about that are always in the midst of some personal drama, it can be a real drain just to spend time with them. I'm not talking about the loyal friend who is just going through a temporarily difficult time but the person that seems to create drama. If things were running smoothly, something would come along to upset the apple cart. You have lots to do – meditate, journal, take care of yourself, build relationships, work. When someone in your life seems to always leave you feeling empty and down, you need to reassess the relationship.

The first person you have to honor is yourself. You need to do what is right for you, in the least disruptive way for the others in your life who are affected. I read a line recently in one of the Conversations with God books that explains it really well: *"Betrayal of yourself in order not to betray another is betrayal nonetheless."*

"Love makes the world go around."

The ultimate opportunity for personal growth is available when we truly commit ourselves to a mate. It's not as easy to detach from the teacher when he or she shares a body with your partner.

When I made the decision to get a divorce, I was naïve enough to think that all I needed to do was find a different person. It was about what he wasn't, rather than about who I was.

I started dating a man that, by all standards, was completely different from my ex-husband. It didn't take long for all the same issues to surface. Here I was living the same life with a new person. The only common denominator was me. No getting around that one!

I have a friend that says denial translates like this: **D**on't **E**ven k**N**ow **I** **A**m **L**ying. The first step to your new life is realizing that it all comes back to you. Nothing changes until you change and, when you change, everything changes.

I had asked my husband many times to go to counseling with me. He wasn't interested, and I was stubborn enough to think I wasn't going to work on it alone. In hindsight, that's the only thing I regret. I should have gone to counseling and dealt with my own issues, whether he wanted to be a part of the process or not. In the end the transition would have been much easier on everyone. If you can get to a peaceful place and know you have really turned over every stone, then it's much easier to let it go.

Once you're ready to move on, you have to be open to the possibilities. Even a creek in the forest starts at nothing! At the top of the mountain, there is creation energy. It starts as a few drops of melting snow or rain. It gathers and forms pools. It cooperates and forms streams. The streams cooperate to form a creek… and eventually a river.

Relationships are like this. In the beginning, there's nothing. You may not even know the person. But one day there's a spark... sometimes spark at first sight! The relationship starts as a few drops of interest and grows into pools of common interest. Then you start to flow together, sometimes more together than separate and sometimes the other way around.

With cooperation and interest, the flow builds to a point where you are much more powerful flowing *with* the person than without. Like a river - so powerful it can carve rocks, create magnificent beauty, feed nature and humans. You can try to control it, to harness its power, but the beauty is in - or a result of - the natural flow. Having said that, I'll also admit that going with the flow is sometimes easier understood than done.

While most people say they want a partner who is their best friend, who flows with them like a river, it often seems nearly impossible to find. Why is that? Let's look at what makes someone a best friend... We would all probably include things like common interests, respect, trustworthiness, fun, and history in our top ten list of best-friend qualities. Are you willing to make time to build these things with your partner? Do you prioritize your time off so that it is spent in joint activities?

It's easy when you're young. When you were in school, your best friend was the person that you could always count on to be your companion in whatever activity you enjoyed. Life tends to complicate things a little, but the same holds true. If you want your partner to be your best friend, you must share companionship.

For example, shopping might be something a female would do with a best friend, so she asks her partner to go with her. He then has several choices. He could choose not to go, instead spending time with someone else (which indicates he is actually creating a best friend in that other person). He can go, begrudgingly, and make everyone miserable. Or he can go just because he wants to spend time with her, in which case her job is to make shopping a pleasant experience. What is it about shopping that he finds unappealing as a way to spend time together? How could she alter the way she shops to make it fun for both of them?

If this feels like a stretch, she might try putting herself in his shoes. Maybe he wants to play golf *and* spend time with her. She has several choices. She could either choose not to play golf (and instead go shopping with someone else, potentially creating a best friend in them). She could join him on the golf course and make it known that she'd rather be shopping, making for a really long day. Or she could approach golfing with an inquisitive mind. What is it about golfing that he really enjoys? How could we make this time together really special?

Of course, I'm not suggesting that you spend time with your partner to the exclusion of all your other friends, but it *is* something you need to think about. Your relationship isn't strong and healthy just because you spend every night sleeping in the same bed. You spend the couple of hours left over before and after work together *because* you are comfortable with that person as a result of the relationship-building you've done at other times and in other ways. When you choose to spend large chunks of your discretionary time without your partner, it only makes sense that the relationship suffers as a result.

The more time you spend together, the better you know each other, and the better friends you will become. It isn't about shopping or golfing; it's about having time to really get to know each other. In other words, it's about nurturing the relationship. You get out of it what you put into it.

Going deeper, you must have trust and intimacy to have a deep, meaningful relationship. If you and your partner agree that this is where you both want to go, you need to be willing and able to expose yourself, to be vulnerable, in order to get to where you want to go. You can't throw something back in your partner's face that he or she has shared with you in a moment of openness and vulnerability. If you do, you won't be fortunate enough to have them open up to you that way the next time. The space that is created needs to be honored.

Best friends are invaluable. To really reap the rewards requires a true commitment to yourself and to each other.

Chapter 16
Problems at the Office

"We're just one, big, happy family."

There is no denying that you spend more time with the people you work with than you do with your family and friends. In such a concentrated environment, it would be unrealistic to think that there would be no disagreements or disputes. In fact, even though you spend very little time with your family and friends, you still have plenty of disagreements and disputes with them.

To begin with, you need to recognize that there are many relationship dramas played out at the office. Issues similar to those you would deal with in sibling rivalries, parenting, and intimate partnerships can all be seen at work. So you need to love your work family unconditionally (or at least aspire to), just like you do your family and friends. This applies to vendors and customers, as well as co-workers.

In any customer service-oriented company (which should be pretty much every company), there will inevitably be a time when you encounter an unhappy customer. No matter what you try to do, it seems to backfire and make matters worse. I have been on both sides of this fence many times. As the company, we have made promises that we may, or may not, have kept. As the customer, my expectations have not been met, and I feel it's important to let the company I'm doing business with know that. When I have a problem with a supplier, I take some time to look at my own expectations. *"Am I in reality?"* Once I know where I'm coming from, then I have to initiate communication with the proper person at the supplier company.

It doesn't really matter which side you're on. In either case, the desired outcome is to try to come to a place of understanding and create a win/win. The quickest way to reach a new level of understanding is to ask yourself how you would feel if you were standing in the other person's shoes. If you can see it through their eyes, you can find a way to bridge the gap. Once you do that, you can apply what you've learned to future situations.

There is tremendous value in positive, long-term relationships. If there is a chance the situation can be turned around, then every stone should be overturned in trying to do that. If continuing the business relationship doesn't work for either party, then you have to be willing to let it go. You just need to give everyone a chance to participate in the decision-making process.

"People who live in glass houses shouldn't throw stones."

No matter who you're dealing with, everyone has qualities that you really appreciate and then some that are a bit trickier to see the beauty in. If you take some time to work with this, you'll see how the traits that bother you most are actually somehow mirroring aspects of yourself. The easiest way to get to this place is to ask, *"How might I have done the same thing this person is doing?"* If you are genuine, it won't take long for something to venture across your screen. You'll see yourself in the other person. And then it will be much easier to get to compassion, empathy, and maybe even understanding.

Your own behaviors may not always be appreciated by those you come into contact with, even though you probably developed them to deal with life. For you, they serve a crucial role in your very survival. When you see yourself in others, you come face to face with what and who you are. If you don't like what you see, you have the choice to do things differently and bless the person that served as your mirror and allowed you to see clearly.

This approach is definitely better than the alternative of gossip, a really dark horse to run with. It seems that the office is potentially where the most damaging gossip occurs, although I'm still speculating on why this is the case. For some reason, all the intolerance and 'better than' attitude that we experienced going through school is carried into our new environment, the workplace.

Whenever you spend time discussing another person's affairs, especially in a business environment, you are playing with fire. You might ask, "What else can I talk about at the water cooler after I get past the weather?" My answer? Talk about yourself or the person you are talking to. If what you are saying about other people couldn't be said to their face, then it's gossip. That makes it pretty simple.

Let's say you're having a conversation with someone and the subject of Betty comes up. If you're praising Betty, saying how wonderful she is and how much you enjoy working with her, then when she walks up, you'd say, "Betty, we were just talking about how wonderful it is to have you around here." That's not gossip.

If, however, Betty comes up and you quickly change the subject or become quiet, then you were gossiping about Betty. Put yourself in her shoes. You know how uncomfortable it makes you when you find out someone has been talking behind your back, so it doesn't make sense to do it to someone else.

If the people that you associate with can't seem to find anything more enlightened to do than gossip about people that aren't present, then I respectfully suggest you find other people to associate with. There's a good chance that, when you're not around, they're gossiping about you too. They're not the people you want as friends.

"One bad apple spoils the whole bunch."

We've all heard the saying about the bad apple. Nowhere is this more true than in the office environment. One discontented employee can bring down the energy of a whole department, which ultimately affects the whole company. You know who these people are. They're the ones that spend their time gossiping and complaining.

Perhaps it's because they feel trapped in a job or work that doesn't inspire them. They have risen to a point where they are making good money, and they can't imagine sacrificing the paycheck for the pursuit of their dreams. To complicate matters further, by the time they get to this place, they usually have several other people more or less dependent on that paycheck too. Other times, it may be their way of dealing with problems, but it is certainly a disruptive way of doing that.

Whatever the cause, gossiping and complaining do absolutely no good and bring everyone down to the level of those who start it. The option is to make a different choice and do something constructive, choosing to spend time working on possible solutions rather than complaining about the current situation. Otherwise, even co-workers eventually tire of hearing the same old story and wish management would take care of it, so everyone could get back to more productive activities.

In this type of stalemate, no one wins. Management usually knows what's going on but isn't sure how others will view a forced separation. Even the discontented employee fails to find anything truly rewarding in their actions. Someone has to make the tough decision. Either a respected employee needs to step forward and bring the situation to light, the company needs to take a chance and force the employee to move on, or the unhappy employee needs to take responsibility for him or herself.

If you recognize yourself as any of the parties mentioned, you have an opportunity to move things along by taking matters into your own hands. Make the tough decision, initiate the difficult discussion, and watch the universe support you in and through it. Again, it's not a matter of standing in judgment; it's still important to see things from the other person's perspective.

We've all experienced something similar. At first, work was something that you liked to do. It was fulfilling and put meaning into your life. In fact, it didn't feel like work at all. You were getting paid to 'play'. You woke up in the morning without an alarm clock. You got out of bed with enthusiasm.

But then, something changed. Somewhere along the road, you grew and the job didn't. Or maybe the job grew, and you didn't. One of the things that really inspired me to write this book was my own experience with this kind of discontent. I finally did give up the paycheck; fortunately, I was the only one dependent on it.

I don't believe it had to be this way. Had I begun practicing the concepts in this book a few years earlier, I am convinced that my work would have grown up around me. I knew what I wanted to do, but I couldn't see how I could do that in the organization I was committed to. In other words, I didn't trust Spirit to work it out in everyone's best interest. The more I dreamed of what I really wanted, the more distant I became.

Every day that you go to work with the mere expectation of meeting the requirements to get your paycheck, the ground under your feet gets less stable. This approach only achieves temporary favorable results. It is slowly killing you and the organization you work for.

So, it's time to retrace your steps. Where did things go astray? More importantly, what can you do today to change things for the better? The easiest thing to change is your own attitude and thoughts. This will quickly result in a very different experience of your work. While you may not be able to see the immediate implications, just moving in the right direction can breathe life into any situation.

With some of the experiences I've had in the last several years, I can see how I might have remained right where I was *and* realized all my dreams. I don't believe that was the right thing for me, but for many others, it can make creating that dream job much less threatening.

Once again, it requires that you accept that you don't know all the possibilities and that you couldn't possibly keep up with all the players. Your real job is only to get to know yourself and then create your perfect paid job in your mind from that knowingness. As long as you do it with purity and ask for only what is in the best interest of all concerned, you can trust that whatever the universe creates will be perfect.

While you're busy dreaming up your new job or duties, work with commitment in your current job. Don't let a day go by that isn't spent creating meaningful work product. Nothing goes unrewarded in the universe. If you give a less than honorable effort today, know that at some point you will be rewarded likewise.

What is considered honorable? You are the judge of that! You know when you aren't doing your best, giving it your all. Since you create your reality, you will attract to yourself exactly what you feel you deserve based on your efforts. Even the most menial tasks can be rewarding, even if not so much in the financial sense.

As an accountant, we spent lots of time in front of a computer. Data entry was considered a more tedious job than filing or answering the phones. When an associate would tell me they just couldn't do data entry, I had a difficult time understanding why. For me, data entry was extremely challenging.

If I was entering checks, for example, I needed to do it fast but with tremendous accuracy. It required my full attention. The better I got at it, the more mistakes I could catch on my way through the process, rather than waiting until I proofed my work at the end. I could catch not only my own mistakes but client mistakes as well. If I did a really good job, I could proof my work and have no mistakes to correct.

You can apply this approach to virtually any job. How can you do it better, faster, more accurately, with more of a customer service focus, and in a way that inspires your own creativity? You have to do it for yourself. It is about loving the work you do and being proud of what you produce. As you do this, you'll find opportunities arising from places you never imagined. You'll find new ways of doing things or solutions to problems that give you a real sense of satisfaction.

In my many years of business management and consulting, I had the opportunity to explore many ways to approach problem-solving and team-building. I was thrilled when an associate would come to me with a problem and sincerely want to be part of the solution instead of merely complaining. It is easy to find all the things that are wrong in a situation or organization, but not so easy to come up with well-thought-out possibilities of ways to right those wrongs.

Any problem is actually a symptom of something that isn't functioning properly. The system has failed and needs to be reevaluated. Sometimes the system just isn't capable of supporting the function that it was originally intended to support and needs to be completely redesigned. When you identify something that you don't like or that isn't working, do you complain about it or do you begin the creative process?

If you want things to change for the better, the choice is yours. One person moving in a new enlightened direction has the ability to bring the energy of the universe along with them.

"All work and no play make Jack a dull boy."

For the most part, people equate productive work with having a paying job. While a paying job is essential for bringing in income, it is also considered a defining characteristic of achieving adulthood. As we become active participants in creating the economy, other aspects of our lives sometimes get short-changed.

Such was the case with a truly delightful person I was fortunate to have the opportunity to work with for most of my years at the helm of the accounting firm. This person came to work every day with a smile on her face and with the intention of being a ray of sunshine in the lives of those she touched. She never did less than her very best. Even in the most stressful times, she managed to maintain her positive and optimistic outlook and sprinkle it onto others. She loved her job, and it showed in everything she did. The only problem was that she loved it a little too much. It consumed her life.

For several years, I tried to discuss with her how better to manage her workload, but she really didn't want to change it. She liked what she was doing and all her responsibilities. As long as she was managing to stay on top of everything (and have an admirable attitude), I decided that I just needed to let her work in whatever way was best for her.

Eventually, it began to fall apart. The example she set was in many ways exemplary, but it made everyone feel like the only way to be successful in the company was to commit your entire life to work. No one else was willing to give that much, and she ended up having to pick up the pieces every time someone gave up. Ultimately, it seemed like the best thing for all concerned was that she take some time to find balance in her life.

She told me once that, if the pendulum swings too far in one direction, it has to swing a bit too far the other way before it can eventually settle in the middle. When work is overemphasized, it manifests just like any other addiction in our lives. It controls us and takes us away from the activities that we say we want to focus on. It leads to imbalance.

I have used the pendulum analogy many times as I watch humans design their lives, realize they've created something that doesn't really serve them, and then re-design a bit too far in the other direction. Whenever I realize that I've stretched myself too thin, I think of the pendulum and try to make minor adjustments so that I don't have to swing too far in the other direction and be back in another uncomfortable position.

Let me give you an example. When I left the accounting firm, I had spent so many years with a rigid schedule that I was unwilling to make an appointment to get my hair cut more than a few days in advance. I wanted the freedom to do what I wanted to do, when I wanted to do it. That was a bit extreme, so I gradually began shifting my mindset along with my scheduling. Now, while I am still very protective of my schedule (and the freedom or lack thereof that it creates), I can make appointments weeks or months in advance without my skin crawling.

More and more people are now recognizing how the traditional work paradigm creates these types of problems and keeps people from becoming whole, well-balanced individuals. As a result, assumptions about jobs are changing, leading to more economically just and personally fulfilling work opportunities for both men and women.

"The times, they are a-changing."

As this new paradigm becomes the norm, new sources of wealth will arise, although you may not easily recognize them because they fall outside of our conventional economic criteria. For example, the Gross Domestic Product (GDP) rises when more people get sick and medical expenditures increase. Yet when people's health care expenditures decline because their health improves, the GDP falls, which supposedly means that society is now producing less wealth. It is obvious that new economic indicators which reflect the value of human and environmental well-being need to be developed, to support the shift to a more humane and just economy.

Organizations also need to adjust. Those which embrace the new paradigm acknowledge the innate human need and desire to do work that: 1) is creative, empowering, self-enhancing, and enjoyable; 2) allows us to connect with and enjoy other people; and 3) makes a positive, recognizable contribution to the world. People don't want to avoid such work; they want to participate in it. And they don't need to be forced to do it; they just need to be allowed to create it.

Because it serves both material needs and non-material values, a work opportunity should promote personal and environmental health and community betterment. Organizational decision-making should be based on what will lead to the best win/win solutions for the company, the workers, the larger community, and the natural environment. The work culture should support and promote self-development, using technology to make work more enjoyable and educational. To allow employees to create a balanced life, jobs should be designed with a healthy, long-term perspective. The new paradigm considers these things, focusing on two major aspects.

1. Greater empowerment — The trend of giving employees more control over their work is seen in organizations everywhere. Employers have discovered that workers who have more say about their job tasks and workplace environments are physically and emotionally healthier and more productive. Progressive businesses have flattened hierarchies, increased employee participation in decision-making, and incorporated spirituality in the workplace.

In fact, some of the nation's largest corporations and most prominent organizations are promoting the use of spiritual techniques and ancient wisdom. Here are just a few examples:

- Xerox employees go on vision quests for inspiration and guidance on product development. Conscious of the potential environmental impact of their products, they commune with nature, taking along only the bare essentials. And they use a ritual similar to Native American talking circles in which a stone is passed around the discussion group and only the holder can speak. This ensures everyone the chance to be heard.

- At a Young Presidents' Organization conference, those attending lay prone and blindfolded, surrounded by the sound of a lone tribal drum and the scent of incense, as they were led through a meditation to connect with their power animals as a means of helping guide their companies to future success.
- Aetna's Chairman spoke to employees about the benefits of meditation and using spirituality in their careers.
- Nationwide, executives regularly attend prayer breakfasts and spiritual conferences.

Spirituality is finally being recognized as critical to a well-balanced existence, and the virtue of ancient wisdom has come to the forefront. This is even true in the work environment itself, as it becomes imperative that the office environment support creativity.

We discussed feng shui in earlier chapters. The application of these principles can have even more dramatic results in the work environment than they do in your personal space. It's all about energy flow. You've been in a company when things just feel good. Everyone is busy, but they don't seem stressed. They're enjoying their work and like to serve.

Companies are learning that it's much easier to create that environment when you start from the ground up. If the lighting, color choices, furniture, and equipment don't help employees get the job done, then they need immediate attention. Printers that keep jamming need to be fixed or replaced. The aggravation and lost productivity cost far more than a printer. It is hard enough to deal with customers, suppliers, employees, family issues, and everything else that is brought to work. There's no reason to make it more difficult.

2. Reduced work hours — Many companies are also exploring ways to reduce work times. By eliminating truly unnecessary jobs and spreading the remaining work around more widely, everyone can spend less time at work. More time for personal, family, and community life also means less stress, better health, and lower health-care costs. This may seem a bit extreme to some, but it's important to keep an open mind.

It's understandable, given these shifts, that there must be some give and take. As the role of business continues to change, large-scale employers may be less able (or willing) to provide everything for their employees that has traditionally been expected. If, as an employee, you want more freedom, less work time, and greater autonomy, then you must assume more responsibility for yourself. This means that you need to make a commitment to learn new skills in order to diversify your abilities, so you will have more to give to yourself and others.

By now, you probably know which areas of your life could use some skill-building. There's no time like the present to do whatever is necessary to acquire new knowledge. And since you probably spend a considerable amount of your waking hours at work, any new skill you add to your tool chest will benefit that area of your life as well. Expanding and sharing your knowledge and abilities is an essential step toward true empowerment.

Chapter 17

How Big Is the Planet?

"Be fruitful and multiply."

Back when the planet had only a few million people on it, a person could build a case for the value of huge families. In the days of Noah and Abraham, the tribe with the largest number of young men was usually the tribe that survived because they had the biggest army. Historically, we've rationalized this dominating lifestyle by focusing on the 'good things' that have resulted from it, namely technological advancement. But now, this approach threatens our very existence.

Global population now increases as much every three days as it did in a whole century for most of the thousands of centuries we've been on Earth. For every additional million people, the added demand on the planet includes not only the land needed to grow enough food for them, but the land taken up by whatever mining, drilling, pumping, and dumping is needed to produce the buildings, streets, vehicles, and everything else used by that many people.

Experts on demographic trends would tell you that the world's birth rates have actually been declining and that the population spike will thankfully peak in another half-century or so and then decline. While the projections show that the population explosion will be done a half-century from now, they ignore the reality of what we will have to go through to get from here to there. The projections turn a half-century of human tragedy into a curve on a graph.

So, if the growing world population and the related use (or abuse) of resources is our biggest problem, how do we control it? Is there something we can learn from those who came before us?

The indigenous tribes knew how to consume resources in a healthy, sustainable way. They did not consume in a way that would destroy their world, even though they had access to far more resources than they used. And while we are led to believe they lived in a crude and desperate style, the historical data simply fails to support that.

These people were profoundly tuned into their environment. They lived a sustainable life, understanding the sacredness of the world and seeing the presence of the Creator and divinity in all things. Their lives were generally quite fulfilling, with far more leisure time than working class citizens of the industrialized world will ever enjoy. But how did these indigenous tribes manage not to overpopulate?

One explanation for how these people controlled their population can be found in the theory that fertility is a function of available food supplies. Research suggests that wild and caged animal populations sustain their population by growing to the capacity of their food supply and then stopping. I have observed this with the fish in my fish tank. The fish grew to an appropriate size for their tank and then stopped. Nobody knows exactly how this happens.

Animals seem to be more aligned with a higher consciousness than we give them credit for. There are examples well beyond population control. When a certain number of birds in England learned how to open the tops of milk bottles left out by milkmen in the 1930's, suddenly birds all over Europe began to do it. The speed with which the behavior was transmitted defies any possibility that one bird had traveled to another and taught it. The English Channel added a further barrier, as these were not migrating birds but smaller than a typical sparrow. There have been similar accounts of non-localized behavior in monkey populations.

"As you sow, so shall you reap."

So, if animals are tuned in to the delicate balance of the universe, much like our ancient ancestors were, where did the human race go astray? Our process of over-consumption began with the discovery of large-scale hunting and fire. With these developments, humans could survive in colder climates, cooking and preserving foods and living in caves during the winter. Since vegetation was absent during the winter, meat probably became a much greater staple of the human diet. This likely led to the destruction of many large animals, causing the first ecological crisis as the human population expanded.

The response to this crisis was to turn to more intensive gathering and preserving of foods, a practice previously ignored. The dependence on vegetable foods precipitated the development of agriculture, and tribal groups began to claim fields as their 'own'. Thus developed the first permanent villages and the first accumulation of wealth. During times of shortage, those who were not as industrious in food accumulation had to submit themselves to the will of the wealthy in order to survive. This was the first step away from nature and towards the belief that nature could and should be dominated.

This led to the world we live in today. Our male-dominant society has embraced the viewpoint that the planet is ours for the taking.

A little bit of history: Male-dominant societies typically have male-only creation stories. In ours, Adam is coerced by Eve, and it is she who is responsible for the fall of man. These roles are then reflected in the culture's belief system.

Women, in this case, are considered consorts of evil gods who must be controlled, hidden, and dominated. The female body is seen as dangerous to male potency. When a conflict arises over resources, the female body becomes the symbolic terrain on which the struggle is acted out. Women, as life-givers, are defined as threats of death. The menstrual blood that for tens of thousands of years was viewed as a sacred substance to sprinkle on fields or to use in fertility ceremonies becomes 'unclean'. The pain experienced during childbirth is offered as proof of woman's errant ways, since 'it must certainly be God's punishment'.

An alternative view of reality is one of gender parity. Societies with gender parity virtually always have creation myths that attribute the creation either to a female or a male and female together. In societies that have achieved gender parity, there is an elaborately-structured mutual acknowledgement of male and female prestige and power. Women concede power roles to men, and men acknowledge that they receive these from women.

While gender parity seems to be the path of choice, we need to recognize how we got here and embrace the lessons learned in the creation of a male-dominant society. To overcome the very real male-female conflict still present in society and promote a society where equality of the sexes and harmony with nature are clear goals, we need to recognize the obligation to raise responsible adult males. Doing so will require a continued shift in parenting. We need to instill more than just an attitude of helpfulness toward females. What we're talking about here is a fundamental reconstruction of the primary roots of culture, transforming the gender imaging of child-parent relationships.

"United we stand, divided we fall."

Human societies have long dealt with the issues most critical to their present survival by telling eye-opening stories. Whether in the form of myths, legends, or songs, these tales either recount prehistoric events that actually occurred or relate some intuitive grasp of what we can bring on ourselves if we disrespect the powers of the universe. These stories offer much more than mere entertainment.

For as long as three hundred thousand years, humans have huddled together in the night to ponder and celebrate the mysteries of the universe. The people told sacred stories of how the world came to be, of what the human brings to the universe, and of what it takes to live a noble life.

Until now… Contemporary humans seem to be the first culture to break with this tradition of celebrating the mysteries of the universe. Those of us, who think earlier cultures knew something important about the universe that completely escapes our way of knowing, are left with a sense of sadness that such experiences are not a bigger part of our lives.

While many of us gather weekly to reflect on our relationship with the divine and participate in a tremendous diversity of religious celebrations, only rarely will we find serious contemplation of primal human questions. The Earth and universe, as they are and actually function, are regarded as 'science', something separate from the questions of the meaning and values that religions deal with.

The birthplace of the universe, where existence first sprang forth, is fifteen billion light-years from the Earth. Most physicists regard this discovery of the birthplace of the universe as the most significant of the twentieth century. Religion prefers to steep itself in the creation myth that provides the basis for the birthplace in the context of its own belief system. It is this divergence that leaves room for an ignorance of the real significance of our impact on the world around us.

"You can't have your cake and eat it too."

Many scholars would agree that Christian fall-and-redemption spirituality is the source of the problem. Essentially a culture of patriarchal oppression and war, followers of Christianity have been taught to look away from the mutable world of nature, with its cycles of birth, death, and regeneration, and the tragic costs of eating and being eaten.

Fundamental religions, while condemning immoral behavior, also assure their believers that whatever happens is destined by God, effectively relieving them of responsibility for any effect they may have on their own destiny. If Armageddon comes, it is God's will, and the implicit consequence is that we don't have to – *and cannot* – prevent Armageddon.

This mindset justifies the rape of the Earth. It's all just temporary anyway, right?! One day soon, fire will fall from the sky, most of the world will be destroyed, and all the 'good' people will be instantly lifted into heaven. Whether or not Armageddon comes, the immediate crisis is upon us as a result of people living their lives as if it is just around the corner.

Similarly, a doctrine tells people what is right or wrong, good or evil, without asking them to exercise their own judgment. This effectively relieves them of responsibility for performing one of the primary tasks of being human – to participate actively in the search for understanding and developing consciousness. The kind of questions that would naturally be posed by an inquisitive mind are discouraged because they can't be adequately answered. As a result, personal power is diminished, and, in effect, the individual is reduced to one of the flock.

The story that permeates our culture is that we're all born evil or stupid. Because of Eve's 'original sin', every person, man or woman, is born tinged with evil and bad judgment. With six billion humans on Earth competing for scarce resources, the notions that, "Everybody does it, everybody is sinful, if we don't do it someone else will, it's still legal anyway" are pervasive. They're viewed as survival rationalizations.

Older cultures view the concept of original sin and man's sinful nature with bewilderment. They are equally baffled by the notion of a God who is hateful and vengeful, and who delights in setting humans up with temptation and then punishing them when they succumb.

These cultures are cooperators, not dominators. They live in harmony with the world around them and see all life as sacred. They value community. *"Whatever we do to nature, we do to ourselves."* There is no concept of a separate nature. We are a part of it.

"Tomorrow is another day."

The problems seem so obvious, yet we manage to keep our heads in the sand and continue to live life as if there were no tomorrow. If we don't see what's happening, if it doesn't touch us personally, then it isn't real. We may be living in an 'information age' with 'information overload' in some sense, but when it comes to what actually gets into people's heads, we're instead living in an age of 'knowledge scarcity'. People no longer know information that is vital to sustain life.

In the tale of the Emperor's New Clothes, each person saw a naked emperor and simply thought this could not be possible. Therefore, they were unwilling to mention what they saw, for fear they would be judged insane. There are six billion of us in a position much like those souls observing the emperor.

We are confronted with something so completely outside our experience that we don't really see it, even when the evidence is overwhelming. Even the most educated, news-watching, world-savvy people among us have only the vaguest awareness of the fact that the most world-changing event in the history of our species is happening right now.

We choose to stay in the comfort of denial. Our mass addictive and self-destructive behavior couldn't possibly be putting our whole world at risk. Addiction keeps a person focused on the immediate experience. It takes many forms: drugs, sex, or television, shopping, gambling, or eating. Addiction is whatever reduces our consciousness and keeps us from expanding our ability to conceptualize, imagine, foresee, or remember.

Our children are initiated into the world through television advertisements. This is how they derive their primary faith. Faith is what a person holds to be their highest truth in their version of reality. Authentic spiritual development is replaced with advertising's materialism. While parents may attempt to give children a spiritual foundation, one hour on the weekend can't possibly make the slightest dent in the strategic bombing taking place day and night, 52 weeks of the year, in front of the television.

At one time, conscious self-awareness was alive only in a tiny fraction of the existing primates. But the destiny of the species was forever altered when this form of consciousness emerged in increasing numbers, until it became the determining characteristic of humanity.

And now, a new form of consciousness is beginning to emerge in a small slice of contemporary humans. As with early self-awareness primates, we are astounded by the new awareness. When we go to speak of it, we discover that we have no easy, established, or efficient way of transmitting this mode of consciousness. By learning the ways of the universe and by reflecting on them as they surface in daily life, we take the first steps into a new form of human understanding and existence.

As we embrace this new understanding, we begin to value the development of consciousness. As a result, a new socio-economic sector, known as cultural creatives, has emerged (as was described in Chapter Two). Culture is not about what is absolute, real, or true. It's about what a group of people gets together and agrees to believe.

In ancient times, people relied on their intuition. It was 'normal' to hear voices and see spirits. The brain was more fully connected. As the use of the written language became widespread, the connection to the right hemisphere of the brain was lost. Only the mystic or schizophrenic had contact with that part of the brain during normal waking consciousness.

Consciousness is not confined to any one place. In fact, it could be that the universe is made of consciousness and nothing else.

Most humans don't live on the Earth that rotates and revolves around the sun. Rather, we live in a fantasy that regards the Earth as a fixed place, where the ground is always stationary. To contemplate the solar system, until you feel the great Earth turning away from the sun and until you feel this immense planet being swung around its massive cosmic partner, is to touch an ocean of wonder as you take a first step into inhabiting the actual universe and solar system and Earth.

Psychological investigators questioned Einstein about his consciousness during moments of radical creativity. Instead of speaking in algebraic formalisms or geometric intuitions, Einstein said his experiences were of 'the muscular type'. He eventually despaired of ever explaining his experience of creativity in a way that others could understand.

How could he explain that he relied primarily on imagination emanating from a state of consciousness that resulted from years of disciplined preparedness? He absorbed what he experienced through feelings in his body that were caused by the energy permeating the universe.

Einstein worked on developing his creative receptivity. When the information was made available to him, he was ready. The most important part of personal transformation is to become fully alive, alert, aware, and conscious of your surroundings and the divinity everywhere. In that way, you are receptive to the messages that the universe needs you to hear.

"You don't get something for nothing."

Our problems arise out of our culture and our view of the world. Only when we change our way of seeing and understanding the world can we produce real, meaningful, and lasting change. That change, in perspective, will then naturally lead us to begin to control our population, save our forests, re-create community, and reduce our wasteful consumption.

It is so easy to get caught up in the political game. In the last election, I found myself voting for a candidate I didn't really believe in because we were told that to vote our conscience would be a vote for the party we least favored. It didn't feel good at the time, and now it seems even illogical. The privilege of voting is our way of letting our voice be heard. I would have been better served by not voting, than by voting for someone I didn't believe in.

While voting on Election Day is a way to influence policies, it is much more powerful to vote with your money. A couple of years ago, I made a decision to invest only in companies that were considered socially responsible. My stockbroker is a good friend, and, after much discussion, she went to work researching the most appropriate funds to invest in. She works for one of the largest brokerage firms, and I was surprised to find that there were not too many funds that were available through her firm that met this criteria. Obviously, not enough people have insisted on investing with their values. Or maybe people haven't clarified what their values are.

Growing numbers of people today are realizing that what we need is not more economic success, but a new definition of what a successful economy can be. The new paradigm recognizes that nature is not merely a collection of passive physical materials waiting to be dug up or chopped down. Rather it is a dynamic living system of plants, animals, soils, waters, weather, and numerous other processes that constitute the ultimate source of all our economic activities. An economic system that honors the Earth is also one that enhances human quality of life.

In Revelations, the Bible commands that we subdue the Earth. It goes further to instruct, "Hurt not the earth, neither the sea, nor the trees." This is a great example of how the Bible becomes the source of much confusion. How do we effectively subdue the Earth if we aren't supposed to hurt it?

The Indians of South America teach us that, to become human, *"One must make room in oneself for the immensities of the universe."* Unless we do, we cannot find our true nature. We will wander in pain and loneliness. Caught in fragments of our nature, we will attach ourselves to one fragment after another, each taking us further away from our center.

No matter how overwhelming the problems of the world may seem, you do have an effect, even if nobody ever knows what you've done. For example, prayer has been demonstrated, in double-blind, scientifically-controlled experiments conducted at Harvard University, to speed healing, even when the people praying and the people healing don't know each other, have never met, and are located in different parts of the world.

How many people will it take to change the world? The organization known as "Only Love Prevails" claims the number is a mere 80,000. They suggest that people should respond to any negative event by mentally chanting, "Only love prevails."

Their premise is based on the physicist's understanding of the laws of wave mechanics. The intensity of waves that are in phase with each other is the square of the sum of the waves. Two waves added together are four times as intense as one wave, ten waves are one hundred times as intense.

Since thought is an energy and all energy occurs as waves, this group believes that 80,000 people, all thinking the same thing together, are as powerful, in terms of creating the reality that we all share, as the 6,400,000,000 people that inhabit the Earth thinking chaotic random thoughts. Therefore, 80,000 people all believing in only love will be enough to change the planetary reality.

Many of us hold very strong values with respect to the environment, planetary healing, world peace, women's issues, spirituality, holistic living, and more. And, while one individual acting alone can certainly make a difference, there are at least 44 million of us who hold similar values. That is an incredible number and certainly a number that could affect dramatic change together. When we acknowledge our numbers and visualize together, we can consciously create this new millennium.

Chapter 18

You Are the S-A-G-E

"The possibilities are endless."

Sage comes from the word *sapere*, to be wise. The dictionary defines a 'sage' as one who has discernment and prudence, proceeds from wisdom, and is well-adapted to the purpose. Whenever you're confronted with a problem or situation that requires your attention, it is helpful to ask yourself, *"What would the sage do now?"* Even if you aren't ready to accept that the sage is within you, ask yourself, *"If I were the sage, what would I do?"* You will find it amazing how this hurdles your subconscious blocks and allows you to embrace your power and potential.

The day I found my diamond ring on the golf course is a perfect example. On that day, *I* was the sage. If you recall, I had lost my ring somewhere during the round, with no idea where, yet found it in a very short time. How was I able to do this?

To start with, I recognized that I needed to *slow* (sit) *down* and ask for help. I *acknowledged the thought* by looking at how I got there and what I really wanted to happen (have the ring be returned to me). I *generated solutions,* trusting that it was entirely possible to miraculously find the ring. When the emotions of the moment had passed, I took time to *evaluate the outcome* so that I could take what I learned forward with me.

In using the S-A-G-E approach for problem-solving, you follow these same basic steps: **S**low down, **A**cknowledge the thought, **G**enerate solutions, and **E**valuate outcomes. The technique incorporates many of the skills and practices you have learned throughout this book. I have had some amazing experiences using this approach for problem-solving, and I am sure you will too. To begin, you first need to achieve the right mindset.

S – Slow Down.

Have you ever felt yourself getting really anxious? You see a light coming through the tunnel, which should indicate to you that there is a train approaching and you need to get out of the way. But, you get so caught up in the anxiety that you can't move. Or you do move, but you wind up right in front of it.

In order to deal with problems like a wise old sage, you need to learn to feel the anxiety in your body and know where that will lead you. Once you can do that, you can slow down and tune in. You already know exactly what you need to do. You just need to tap into that knowledge.

One of the ways you resist slowing down and intentionally taking steps towards your desired outcome is to get caught up in the frenzy of life. You buy into the illusion that there isn't enough time to do everything you need to do. In reality, there is plenty of time. It is a matter of prioritizing and accepting that whatever you accomplish is exactly what you are supposed to accomplish. That doesn't mean you sit on the sofa and watch television. The focus here is on mindfulness, not mindlessness. You will be ready to take action as soon as you have dissipated the anxiety.

The boiling point is the place in yourself that reacts whenever you feel overwhelmed by a situation. For me, I can feel the anxiety building. In my former life, I would spin when this happened. I couldn't sit still. I had to do something. More often than not, what I would do would make matters worse. Now, I recognize the feeling and use it to my advantage. It is really trying to tell me something. There is something not quite right (or maybe even *really* wrong) about the situation I'm facing.

Spiritual practices, like meditation, provide me with the perfect tools to dig around and figure out what's going on. Meditation is practiced in many different ways. If you just don't feel like you can settle down on a cushion and quiet your mind, then put on a good pair of walking shoes and hit the pavement. I have solved the problems of the world this way.

You might feel like there is no time to go out for a walk, but I know from experience that the alternative is spending lots of time unraveling the results of bad decisions. What you need is an attitude adjustment. Ask and you shall receive. The universe will send you just what you need.

The most important thing is to constructively dissipate the energy in the situation. In astrology, we know that excessive energy is a sign that Mars is involved. Mars wants you to take action – right NOW! But, you know from experience that the best course may not have presented itself yet. Since you want to take the most direct route, you need to calm Mars down and take your time planning your course. The most effective way to use Mars' energy is to be physically active. That means some form of exercise. Even if your only option is a treadmill in a gym, you will find that, after a good 30 minutes of physical activity, things feel much more manageable.

Another way you can slow yourself down so you can tune in is by using a short relaxation exercise. The one I have included here is taken from the teachings of Swami Sathvananda Sarasuati in his book Yoga Nidra. It takes about 10 minutes and is guaranteed to shift your perspective. You can read this meditation into a tape recorder, pausing at the dashes, and play it back when you need help moving your active mind out of the way.

Lie or sit down in a comfortable position. Take several deep breaths and begin.

Rotation of Consciousness

Go to your right hand and relax your thumb – second finger – third finger – fourth finger – fifth finger – palm of the hand – back of the hand – wrist – lower arm – elbow – upper arm – shoulder – armpit – right ribcage – waist – hip – thigh – knee – shin – calf – ankle – heel – sole – top of the foot – big toe – second toe – third toe – fourth toe – fifth toe.

Go to your left hand and relax your thumb – second finger – third finger – fourth finger – fifth finger – palm of the hand – back of the hand – wrist – lower arm – elbow – upper arm – shoulder – armpit – left ribcage – waist – hip – thigh – knee – shin – calf – ankle – heel – sole – top of the foot – big toe – second toe – third toe – fourth toe – fifth toe.

Go to your right toes – left toes – right sole – left sole – right heel – left heel – right ankle – left ankle – right calf – left calf – back of the right knee – back of the left knee – back of the right thigh – back of the left thigh – right buttocks – left buttocks – small of the back – right rib cage – left rib cage – right shoulder blade – left shoulder blade – right shoulder – left shoulder – back of the head – back of the neck – crown of the head – right eyebrow – left eyebrow – the space between the eyebrows – right eye – left eye – right ear – left ear – right cheek – left cheek – right nostril – left nostril – tip of the nose – upper lip – lower lip – chin – jaw – throat – right collar bone – left collar bone – right chest – left chest – middle of the chest – navel – abdomen – right thigh – left thigh – right knee – left knee – right shin – left shin – right ankle – left ankle – right foot – left foot – whole right leg – whole left leg – both legs together – whole right arm – whole left arm – both arms together – whole back – whole front – whole back and front together – the whole body together – whole body – whole body – whole body.

This meditation is subtle and powerful. By the time you have rotated through your whole body, you will consciously feel whole.

Once you relax and tune in, your greatest desire can manifest as fast as you can conceive of it happening. That usually means it takes a long time. We have a really hard time believing that something that has eluded us for years could literally be a reality in the blink of an eye. Would we really appreciate it if it happened that quickly?

I talked early on about the importance of the process. That's what we're really here for. If we went from a hint of something we're thinking we might possibly want directly to having it now, we humans wouldn't get much joy or satisfaction from it. It doesn't have to be that way; we have chosen to make it that way. The more comfortable you get with the principles presented in this book, the easier it is to skip much of the tail-chasing between desire and manifestation.

I know I'm on the right track when my direction is confirmed by many sources. When I felt ready for a major change in my life several years ago, everywhere I turned there was some form of message that, when I leaped, the net would appear. It took me a couple of years or more to trust that. Now when I get a clear, confirmed message, I am much quicker to act on it.

A – Acknowledge the Thought.

I love to watch my thoughts. Sometimes I'll be driving along and notice that I have just thought about someone pulling out and hitting me. Now anyone who knows about the power of the mind knows this is a dangerous thought. The thought oozes out, but fortunately I catch it. After a moment of examination to see if there is any value in it, I wave my hand to the left across my face and say, *"Cancel that."* I have just sent a clear message to my subconscious that I don't intend to put any energy into manifesting that thought. What would have happened if I hadn't cancelled the thought? There's no way of telling if, in fact, someone would have pulled out and hit me, but I'd rather not test the waters.

I do feel confident that your thoughts create your reality. If you allow negative thoughts to permeate your life, you will experience negativity. The amazing result of using this process will be evident as you start to notice your positive thoughts emerging subconsciously. I automatically assume that the best will happen, as opposed to the worst. Even when I am experiencing a difficult situation, I have enough experience to know that the outcome will be perfection. I simply reinforce it by reading an affirmation for use in this type of situation, something like, *"I can hardly wait to see what good comes from this situation."* When I use that phrase, I create the expectancy of a good surprise for myself.

Yet, some of us have minds that work overtime. While that can be a blessing at times, it can also be a curse. I have spent many nights lying awake filtering through possibilities. If I really want to get back to sleep, I need to get up and process whatever I'm facing.

My preferred method of doing this is to take a walk or hike. At 2:00 a.m., that isn't always a reasonable alternative. The next best method is writing; a few pages in my journal and I have tamed the tiger. I can go back to sleep and trust that the light of day will give me a whole new perspective. If what I was so concerned about is really that critical, it will certainly be there in full force the next morning.

It hasn't failed me yet. By the next morning, the situation has come into the light. I can see things much more clearly and usually know just what I need to do. Sometimes, the answer is still to do nothing. Other times, I get a clear message that I wasn't at all expecting (or might not even want to hear), and I ask for confirmation. When it comes from a source that has no idea what it's really confirming, it's pretty much undeniable that you are being led. If you're still uncomfortable, take a small step in that direction and see what surfaces. If you're moving in the right direction, it will unfold effortlessly.

G – Generate Solutions.

It's human nature to want to *do* something when facing a dilemma. I find the easiest way to use that energy is to generate possible solutions. Let's say you have a financial situation that is troubling you. You have no idea *how* this will be resolved, but your spiritual foundation allows you to trust that it will be. In order to get past the 'how now' drain, try sitting down and writing your way through it.

There are truly unlimited possibilities for the ultimate outcome. If you can come up with one or two ways that the universe might work things out, then you can let it go and detach from the situation. Sometimes, you really have to stretch to come up with a possible solution. You need to dream big, so even winning the lottery is a potential solution. No one ever really expects to win the lottery, but it has to happen to someone. Why not you?

So let's say you've come up with one or two possible solutions to your current dilemma. If you're a get-to-work person like me, you want to put a plan into action right away. That's not the point of coming up with possible solutions though. All you're really trying to do is keep yourself busy so the universe has time to work. You need to occupy yourself so you don't worry and put fear energy into the situation. I have been shown so many times how worry is a complete waste of my time. How many times do I have to wait to 'get it' after the fact in order to learn to trust it from the moment of conception?

Ultimately, you want to get out of the way and give the universe plenty of room to maneuver. The best way to do this is to take your own energy off of it. You give the universe a clear message with your desire. You let go and trust that it will be resolved. And you get on with the business at hand.

The way I have learned to trust the process is by looking at the outcome and really seeing how the solution that manifested was better than I could have imagined. There are usually many components to the solution and many areas of your life that are affected. If you really look at all the implications, you will be in awe.

It's really easy for me to accept that Spirit is smarter than I am. Why would I think that I alone could even come close to solving a problem with all the interrelationships perfectly folded into it? Even if I thought I could, why would I want to? It is so much easier to let the universe do the hard work. It's sort of like using a computer.

My background is in accounting. I was one of the first people to bring a computer in-house to process tax returns. Still, there was something scary about putting the numbers into boxes and just trusting that the tax return would spit out correctly. If you changed one number, it could result in endless changes to other numbers in the tax return. In the 'old days', when we used to prepare returns by hand, we would go over and over them to ensure accuracy. Today, almost 20 years later, we assume the computer is right, even if we think it's wrong. More often than not, if we start reading the instructions (which even the most typical accountant you can imagine avoids if at all possible), we find that indeed the computer has calculated things properly. So will Spirit calculate things properly for your path.

When you don't get a clear message on what to do next, it's time to let go. I turn it over to Spirit and go to the movies. This is very powerful for me. When I go to the movies, I am completely out of touch. No phone, no computer, no commercials… just pure entertainment without distractions. This is my way of sending the universe a clear message: *"I don't know what I'm supposed to do. I am not going to do anything until I am confident that I'm putting my energy in the direction that will get me where I say I want to go."*

So, you've come up with your possible solutions, and you've turned it over to the universe to solve the problem: *"Spirit, you're smarter than I am, you figure it out. Give me a definite lead and let me know if there is anything I need to do."* All you have to do now is pay attention – and practice patience.

This is why I say my life is like a treasure hunt. The signs and messages are everywhere… on a billboard or the side of a bus, in the words of a song, or from a brief encounter with someone. The other evening, I turned on the television, (which by now you know I rarely do), and the newscaster was talking about candle safety. There was something that demanded my attention, even though I burn candles all the time and have never concerned myself with leaving them burning even when I leave the house.

I actually had two candles that had been burning for several days at the time, and I decided I needed to take a look and make sure I was comfortable that they weren't a hazard. One of the candles seemed to be begging for a little attention, and so I found a dish to put it in. The next morning the candle had burned down and was a pool of wax in the bowl but still burning. *"Wow! Am I glad I paid attention! Thank you, God."*

In the midst of a lengthy meeting later in the day, I heard a crash. The candle had burned through the dish and had started a fire on my desk. The glass top on my desk had shattered, and there were ashes everywhere. It looked a little like a volcano erupted.

Stopping to reflect, I realized how amazing it was that I was warned that the candle would be a problem. I just didn't take it quite seriously enough. I also had a meeting that was supposed to have taken me away from the office but was postponed. Had I not been there, what would have happened?

Whenever I pray, I give thanks for this type of divine guidance and protection. I ask that I be given definitive leads so that I know exactly what I need to do. My job is to watch and listen! Every message and messenger is important. You just need to take time to receive what you need to receive and then take appropriate action.

But what about when you're expecting a solution to a problem, and it doesn't show up? When you really trust that everything is working out perfectly, you know that if something doesn't fall into place, then it isn't right. There are lots of reasons why this might happen. Did you back the universe into a corner? Perhaps the way you wanted the situation to work out would have turned out to be detrimental to one or more affected parties. Maybe since you developed your possible solutions, you've lost interest in the situation. The timing might not be right. Remember, the universe is orchestrating the perfect outcome. I can't even imagine juggling all the components required to pull something like this off myself.

It is, however, fair to ask, "Why not?" I usually get a very clear answer, not always what I want to hear. Maybe I'm somehow not fully prepared for what is coming. I haven't asked for what is truly for my highest good. If you ask for your desired outcome or something better to manifest, under grace in a perfect way, you need to accept the outcome. If you can't get what you want without trouble you weren't expecting, then wouldn't you be glad it never manifested? You have no way of knowing the problems you've avoided by trusting the universe to assist you with the issues at hand.

E – Evaluate the Outcome.

A couple of years ago, I was refinancing a building that I own. I made it so much more difficult than it had to be. The universe had already laid it out. If I had just done what was asked of me and worked in cooperation with the process instead of fighting it, it would've been so much easier! This was one of the countless times I have fretted over how something would resolve itself, only to be amazed at the brilliance of the universe's plan. When the solution manifests, I take some time and really enjoy going back over the experience noticing how perfectly all the pieces fit together.

After the fact, there is tremendous value in reflecting on the outcome. I look for answers to questions like, *"Why did this happen, and what do I need to learn from it?"* If you accept that you have chosen to experience certain situations in this lifetime, then you know that the same issue will present itself again, with a different face on a different stage, if you don't learn what you need to learn from the current situation. Sometimes it is so similar when it resurfaces that there is no way to deny that there must be something you're not getting. This is the point where you know you've got some digging to do in the basement of your subconscious.

Feng shui teaches us that clutter blocks energy flow. When there are issues that you haven't dealt with, they manifest as blocks. You're not really going any further until you get through this lesson. Once you accept that, it's easy to go into it. Wouldn't you rather get it over with now, so you can move on to what you really say you want to do, be, or have?

You already know what to do. The sage is in you, waiting to be embraced. It will be proven to you many times over that before you have asked, you have been answered. The intelligence of the universe is permeating your entire life. All you need to do is connect with your senses.

Chapter 19

Odds and Ends

In southeast Texas, I spent the early years of my life at my grandparents' house. My grandfather was a master gardener. He spent many years working on the mini-farm that consumed the large back yard of their property. When it came time for dinner, we went to the garden to pick fresh vegetables. He worked tirelessly, making his own compost and tending to every detail in the garden and greenhouse. Several years after he and my grandmother had passed away, my uncle reported that there were still tomatoes growing in the garden that were far superior to anything you would find in a store or even at a farmer's market. The ground my grandfather had spent so many years perfecting was still yielding the fruits of his labor.

As I relived my experiences while writing this book, I realized how many moments like this have presented themselves as metaphors for the way I've learned to approach life. They served to show me how I might alter things to get more out of my experiences. As I shared them with you, I reached a point where I had to ask, "Did all of this really happen?" Amazingly enough, the answer was, "Yes." Actually, I had to choose the experiences that I shared, because miracles happen in my life every day.

I believe this is the case because, like my grandfather and his garden, I have put so much energy into recognizing them and cultivating the territory in which I live. When the soil is well prepared, the garden yields far superior results. The tools and concepts discussed in this book help you tend the garden of your mind. The more energy you contribute, the more juicy the results.

So many times, we are too busy chasing the dream to enjoy the fruits of our labor. At some point, a priority shift needs to occur. By consciously choosing where you engage your energy, you can accomplish much more in a shorter period of time. If you are engaging in activities that are aligned with your personal values and goals, then even work becomes fun. There isn't as much focus on how many hours are committed to work but rather how it contributes to joy and satisfaction in your life. You begin taking time to appreciate the little things along the way.

One weekend, I traveled to Sedona, Arizona, with a couple of friends. We hiked up the mountain in Boynton Canyon to visit the Indian ruins. I clearly understood what it meant to stop and smell the roses, yet I hadn't made that a priority. In our rush to climb the mountain, we missed some of the ruins. When I reached the top and realized the significant parts of the experience we had missed, I was deflated. I obviously needed to rethink my priorities. I realized that I was quite effective at climbing to the top. The key observation came when we got there and looked around. It didn't take long to say, "What's next? Was this really a success?"

We all want to live a successful life. Yet success is a very personal thing. It is defined on an individual basis. One person's flaw is another's individual expression of perfection. As you develop your primary relationship, with yourself, you will define what success looks like for you and create your own individual expression of perfection.

It's also rewarding to develop a support system of people that you can share experiences with. These are people that, after listening to you relate your experience, respond with "Amazing!" or "Good job!" Someone that responds "Unbelievable!" creates just that. If they can't believe it, it can't happen. Surround yourself with people who display the characteristics that you want to display. Then, be the greatest version of yourself with them. This way, you can constantly give each other the encouragement to rise to new heights as you experience the complex adventure of life.

Life *is* difficult and complicated, and we have chosen for it to be that way. Take a sporting event, for example. If one team blows the other away, effectively defeating the competition with little effort, it isn't nearly as satisfying as it is when the victory is the result of a hard-fought battle. The fun you experience is directly proportionate to the challenges you overcome. And the challenges you deal with have been created especially for you, customized to the level you are prepared to work on. In other words, when the student is ready, the lesson appears (along with the teacher or person the universe has charged with presenting it).

When I imagine how a sage would deal with a problem, the picture that comes to mind is that of an older person who is obviously unaffected by the situation. The face embodies a smile full of wisdom… not a smirk indicating contempt, but a loving expression. The sage knows there are no circumstances that fail to serve a useful purpose. When confronted with what might be considered a 'problem', the sage delights in the discovery process of life. With the tools you have gathered together in your tool chest (meditation, journaling, anxiety management, etc.), you can be the sage in your own life.

Almost a decade after I lost my ring on the golf course, I moved into a home that I was remodeling. If you recall, this is the home with the clogged bathroom drain. It was summertime, and I made sure I was away for extended periods of time, to avoid the Las Vegas heat and the discomfort of remodeling.

While I usually kept my 'good' jewelry in the bathroom drawer (I wore it less and less over the years because it didn't seem to fit with my new life), I decided it would be safer hidden away while I was gone. The last time I saw the ring, I was putting it away with my watch and bracelet in a special hiding place. I recall trying to be really clever in finding a good place to put them.

Several months later, when I tried to remember where that place was, I drew a blank. I tried not looking, thinking it would just come to me. Then, I tried putting diligent effort into the search. It didn't matter what approach I took, I could never quite muster the same level of desire to find it that I had the day on the golf course. The jewelry no longer held the same meaning for me. There are other interesting details and lessons I learned from the search process, but to make a long story short, I never did find the jewelry.

By this point in my life, though, I knew it had little to do with whether or not I *could* find the jewelry. Literally anything is possible when you tap into the special manifesting powers of the universe. But to get there, everything has to be in alignment – most importantly, your intention and desire. While I wanted to find the jewelry, mostly because I didn't want to file a large claim with my insurance company, I couldn't muster the energy of desire that would have been necessary to walk between the worlds where my jewelry would no doubt have been quite easily found.

The sage lives between the worlds. If you follow the sage's footsteps, you can anticipate miracles at every turn. When you live with intention (knowing what you want) and attention (the focus you put on making it happen), you learn to expect something wonderful to manifest. Ask yourself, "What would the sage do now?", and prepare yourself for the magickal adventure that will surely follow.

Resources

REFERENCES

The following books were used as reference materials in the writing of What Would the Sage Do Now? These works are excellent resources for further studies in the areas of sustainability, healing, and the use of ancient wisdom.

Ayres, Ed (1999). God's Last Offer. Four Walls Eight Windows.

Brandt, Barbara (1995). Whole Life Economics. New Society Publishers.

Cayce, Hugh Lynn (1964). Venture Inward. Harper & Row, Publishers.

Cleary, Thomas (1992). The Essential Confucius. Castle Books.

Collinge, M.P.H, Ph.D., William (1996). Complete Guide to Alternative Medicine. Warner Books, Inc.

Epstein, D.C., Donald M. (1994). The 12 Stages of Healing. Amber-Allen Publishing.

Hartmann, Thom (1999). The Last Hours of Ancient Sunlight. Harmony Books.

Hay, Louise L. (1982, 1984). Heal Your Body. Hay House, Inc.

Levine, Frederick G. (1988). The Psychic Sourcebook. Warner Books, Inc.

Monte, Tom (1993). World Medicine: The East West Guide to Healing Your Body. Putnam Publishing Group.

Morton, Mary and Michael (1996). Five Steps to Selecting the Best Alternative Medicine. New World Library.

Myss, Ph.D., Caroline (1996). Anatomy of the Spirit. Three Rivers Press.

Reilly, Dr. Harold J. and Brod, Ruth Hagy (1975). Health Through Drugless Therapy. A.R.E. Press.

Rossbach, Sarah (1983). Feng Shui: The Chinese Art of Placement. Penguin Books.

Ruether, Rosemary Radford (1992). Gaia & God. Harper Collins.

Seymour, Dr. Percy (1992). The Scientific Basis of Astrology. St. Martin's Press.

Swimme, Brian (1996). The Hidden Heart of the Cosmos. Orbis Books.

RECOMMENDED READING

Several books have had a tremendous impact in my spiritual growth and development. I consider these four, in particular, as required 'life reading' and highly recommend them to you for guidance on your journey.

Cameron, Julia (1992). The Artist's Way. Penguin Putnam, Inc.

Chopra, Deepak (1994). The Seven Spiritual Laws of Success. Amber-Allen Publishing and New World Library.

Gunaratana, Henepola (1991). Mindfulness in Plain English. Wisdom Publications.

Shinn, Florence Scovel (1925). The Game of Life and How to Play it. DeVorss & Company, Publisher.

Index

A

B

C

D

E

F

G

H

I

J

K

L

M

N

O

P

R

S

T

U

V

W

Z

Notes

Notes